Beating
the
Competition

Beating the Competition

150 Ways to Win New Customers for Your Small Business

Tait Trussell

MADISON BOOKS

Published by Madison Books
4720 Boston Way
Lanham, Maryland 20706

Distributed by National Book Network

The paper used in this publication meets the minimum
requirements of American National Standard for
Information Sciences—Permanence of Paper for
Printed Library Materials, ANSI Z39.48–1984. ∞™
Manufactured in the United States of America.

Library of Congress Cataloging-in-Publication Data
Trussell, Tait, 1925–
Beating the competition : 150 ways to win new
customers for your small business / Tait Trussell.
p.   cm.
1. Small business—Management.   2. Customer
relations.   I. Title.
HD62.7.T72   1992
658.8—dc20   92–28459 CIP

ISBN 0–8191–8617–1 (pbk. : alk. paper)

CONTENTS

Introduction

You are about to find out how to accomplish the following:
- Save thousands of dollars in advertising, public relations, promotional, and marketing costs.
- Boost your sales.
- Fix firmly in the public mind a favorable image of your organization.
- Enjoy increasing income by winning new customers.
- Get a leg up on your competition.

You won't fully realize all these rewards, of course, until you have put to use in your own organization at least some of the ideas and strategies I describe in this book.

I can assure you that the potential to beat the competition and win new customers is there for the taking. The reason you will be able to win new customers, impress old customers, save money, and build more profits while feeling more comfortable about your place in the public eye is because the counsel in this publication is a distillation of advice with proven results.

If you are like most business and professional people, you are enthusiastic about your operation. You want to tell the world about it. This publication will tell you how, at least how to tell your world of potential customers. It is packed with money-making strategies and it describes how you can spread the word in believable ways about what you have to offer.

You could go to a high-priced public relations firm to seek the kind of advice this publication offers. But you would have to pay many thousands of dollars for it. And you still might not get the guidance in the easy-to-apply form that this publication offers.

Moreover, you probably wouldn't get the breadth of ideas. Why? Because this book is a compact report not only of my ideas but also of the thinking of many experts—the fruits of years of experience and carefully acquired expertise of respected practitioners and business people.

Using the Guide

If you plan to turn this manual over to someone else in your organization—someone assigned to promote your business, to deal with the news media, and to handle advertising, marketing, or related functions, you really should read the publication yourself first. It will take the thinking of the boss, the person who makes the important final decisions in an organization, in order to make the most of this guide book.

If you yourself will be implementing the recommendations in this publication, you should be relieved to know that you don't have to be an expert in public relations techniques to benefit. Almost anyone with good sense can put the advice into practice with gratifying results.

Even if you don't use all the advice in this book, if you thumb through it your eye will catch many an idea that you or your people can put to use, and use right away.

This guide does represent much of my own thinking and experience in running multi-million dollar public relations and advertising operations in several different fields and working with some of the most demanding clients you could imagine. Fortunately, my background also has been in journalism, sales, and marketing. So, the book is written from a rather broad perspective.

Revealing Trade Secrets

I'm going to reveal a few trade secrets that most people in the business of public relations and image building like to keep to themselves. I will also knock down a few myths that have grown up and misled business people about public relations and the news media.

As you read, you also may learn things about yourself that you hadn't realized before and things about your customers which will help you to understand better why they behave as they do. The publication also will cite some major trends for the future which you will need to know about to be prepared.

By using this manual to impress and win new customers or clients— those you do business with—you won't have to spend years of hit and miss, trying to find the best way to promote your operation.

Easy to Use

The book has been organized so that it is easy to use. The examples and advice will be down to earth and readily adaptable to your own circumstances.

In reading this publication, you may come across an idea or a strategy that will make you say to yourself: "Well, that's obvious." But the simple and obvious are often overlooked or forgotten in the rush of the day's business. Sometimes the simplest idea works best because of its sheer simplicity.

Or you may think to yourself: "That would never work." But, I can assure you what I set forth has worked well for many.

This book offers scores of ideas related to saving and making money. The topics covered include public relations, advertising, promotion, image molding, marketing, and credibility building. And, a few insights that only years of experience in creative work can provide.

If all this has the ring of over promising, it didn't to some of my business friends I let read this guide before final publication. They told me they'd order copies as soon as it was printed.

Remember, there are plenty of businesses that have struggled along and survived even with faulty budgets, or low financing, or average products, or unimaginative marketing, or even slip-shod service. But a business without customers is doomed.

So, read on. And get ready for some eye-opening advice. Good luck and good fortune to you as you win many new customers, the key to beating the competition.

Chapter 1

Our Visibility Society

"The public be damned."

It's hard to believe that anybody in business, much less a famous American industrialist like Cornelius Vanderbilt, would say such a thing. But he did.

How times have changed. Today, we live in what some call the Information Society. I call it the Visibility Society.

No person offering goods or services to the public can escape visibility. Either you look good—you are perceived as running a worthwhile operation and people want to do business with you—or you appear to be stuck in the mud, or worse.

But how does one business manage to look good and another—even one offering the same services, products, or merchandise—fall short?

Mark Twain once said, "Many a small thing has been made large by the right kind of advertising."

Yes, advertising can help. But the key words are "right kind," and although advertising is usually a necessity today, other forms

1

of image building can get you more for your money, particularly "the right kind." But more about that later. First, let's get straight what we're talking about.

Getting Terms Straight

The terms "advertising," "public relations," "marketing," and "promotion" unfortunately are sometimes misused or even used interchangeably.

Advertising is a form of marketing communications that creates awareness of a company, product, or service and its benefits. You have to pay to get it. But you can channel it to targeted audiences.

Public relations has been defined in many ways. I like to think of it as putting your best foot forward in every feasible way. Publicity is a major form of public relations and typically comes free. PR, as public relations is commonly called, tries to link what an organization does with the public interest as well as to earn public acceptance.

The term promotion is sometimes used in a very general sense to encompass any form of communication to make you look good. Sales promotion, more specifically, offers incentives to buy, often to both consumers and to the trade—through coupons, gifts, or contests.

Marketing is the most general term for promoting and selling products and services. Public relations, advertising, and sales promotion are the tools used to advance your marketing purposes and win new customers.

When you are exposed to the public—in this Age of Visibility— people's perceptions can be bad as well as good, of course. The people at Exxon USA can tell you about it as a result of the 1989 Alaska oil spill.

So can the folks who make Perrier, after benzene was discovered in their water. Or McDonald's before it abandoned its polystyrene containers for hamburgers. And even the New England Patriots Football Team.

Remember when the Patriots management was fined $50,000 by the NFL Commissioner, as well as were three of the Patriot players, after one player displayed his nakedness to a woman sports reporter in the locker room after a game? The Patriots got a ton of bad press.

What was particularly pertinent about the fine for the Patriot's management was that $25,000 of it was ordered to be spent for counseling in news media relations. I'm going to tell you later what the Patriots Management should have known about dealing with the press. Bad publicity is incredibly costly and can even wreck a business.

Look what happened to the apple growers when Alar, the chemical they used on the fruit, was branded as a cancer causer. Even though scientific studies later showed that Alar was relatively safe, the damage was done because the scare story was in all the papers and was broadcast everywhere. The apple growers lost millions.

This book will deal with major aspects of marketing, but it will concentrate more on public relations and image building, because I am convinced this has the most long-run potential for saving you money and winning new customers and beating the competition.

Touting the Well Shaped

Public relations has been around for a long time in one form or another. When Great Britain took over Florida from Spain in 1763, the British knew they had to attract investors and settlers to that little known peninsula.

To tout the place, the Brits put out the word that:

"The women are very handsome, and well-shaped...The Floridians...are brave, good-natured people, very hospitable to strangers, and not cannibals, as first represented."

Public relations began by getting people to have favorable opinions about organizations, people, or things. In business, John

D. Rockefeller, the oil magnate and philanthropist, benefited from creative efforts of the man known as the father of business publicity. He was Ivy Lee, and he crusaded for keeping the public informed.

Of course, both advertising and public relations have now become quite sophisticated and efficient. Advertising can pinpoint a specific audience and communicate to that audience in a vast variety of ways.

Deluge in the Future

In the future, we are sure to be bombarded by ads on everything from receipts at the supermarket to subliminal messages on TV.

Public relations, too, will take on new shapes and sizes. Handled the right way, it can now gain support for a business, organization, or cause and send persuasive messages to a host of publics. These include employees, government policymakers, investors, and the news media, as well as the local community and potential customers.

In the future, public relations may well replace much of the advertising as businesses find new ways of using information through means ranging from third-party endorsements to telecommunications to linkages with causes that are admired and supported by the public.

The public, and your customers, are becoming more sophisticated, as well, and more skeptical. So, you will need to know how to meet this challenge.

Both advertising and public relations are taking advantage of remarkable advances in communications technology. This has attuned people to expect immediate information. But more later about how you can benefit from new technology and techniques, too.

Age of the Unexpected

We also now live in an age of the unexpected. Who could have predicted the fall of the Berlin Wall as short a time as a few months before it happened? Or a war in the Middle East after we thought a new era of peace had arrived? Or the breakup of the Soviet Union? Or that a Supreme Court nominee might almost fail confirmation because of a charge of sexual harassment. And we all know how fast commercial fads and products come and go.

As New York baseball great Yogi Berra said: "The future ain't what it used to be."

Business people typically are used to controlling their operations and being able to plan and get measurable results. But events and society are now more unpredictable.

You have to worry about crime and drugs in the workplace, and politicians catering to those who want more and expensive regulations slapped on your business, and people everywhere rebelling against the decline in service, and poorly educated employees, and fickle customers, and the state of the economy, and the impact of international events.

You also have to worry about the growth of unpredictable radical groups, from ultra environmentalists to animal rights fanatics, to critics of the whole concept of the enterprise system. Many critics are well organized and well funded and can make an honest business enterprise appear to be a greedy, thoughtless violator of the public welfare. You may well have to deal with crisis communications one day. I provide pointers on that subject later. (See Appendix E for ways to deal with trouble.)

Major events and trends and even threatening circumstances can sometimes bring major opportunities, if you know how to use them to your advantage. More later also on how you can do this.

In the following chapters, you will learn what I believe are the best and most time-tested ways to impress customers, both new and old customers; and you will read about scores of ideas you will want to try out.

Top Priorities

I probably would insult you to suggest that before you launch any new public relations, advertising, or promotional effort, you must have in mind clearly what special benefits you provide to your customers and a clear picture of your markets. But, strangely enough, some small, and not so small, entrepreneurs charge ahead pell mell without keeping benefits and markets as top priorities in their game plan.

One initial and fundamental warning I would give though is to remember that the truth is always the ceiling above which no amount of advertising or public relations can rise, no matter how flashy or ingenious.

Now, in the next chapter, you'll see how you can lay the solid foundation for your new strategy to create the image that will impress your customers. As the poet Auden counseled, don't look back, "the future shall fulfill a surer vow."

Chapter 2

Getting Where You Want to Go

"What good is geography anyway," the boy griped to his teacher. "As soon as I memorize some country, they pick it up and move it or it changes its name."

Fast-changing international developments and national events. Shifting fads and trends. Unexpected happenings. The economy in flux.

You just can't count on anything remaining the same these days. But even though we can't control change, we can minimize its effect—with a plan.

As in geography, you need a map—and a current one—to know where you are and where you want to go. Obviously you can't win new customers without mapping out your plans for how you're going to do it, for how you will communicate most effectively with them.

What is a communications plan? It's a detailed set of programs or projects, events or actions (preferably in writing) to be undertaken within specified time and cost limits to achieve identifiable results.

If that sounds a bit technical, don't worry. Planning is nothing new for you. You undoubtedly have a business plan, whether it's formal or informal, intuitive or subconscious. You have a pretty good idea of where you want your business to go this year, next year, and into the future.

Well, any communications effort (I use the term "communications" to encompass public relations, advertising, promotion, and image-building) needs its own plan.

Why Start with a Plan

I'll tell you why you need to start with a plan. The nature of communications is intangible. It deals mainly with the transfer of information, with people's attitudes and emotions, and with perceptions that result from the communications. So, by its nature, communications is not easy to grab hold of or to quantify.

In fact, the communications process eludes two traditional measurements of value that businesses typically use: return on investment and productivity.

The return on investment from communications—whether its advertising, public relations, or a related function—can seldom be tied directly to sales volume, even though it can have enormous impact on sales and other important yardsticks of success.

Likewise, the standard definition of productivity—units of output divided by units of input—can't be applied easily. Communications (especially public relations) is never precise in terms of measurable output, even though sometimes a small amount of brilliant input can produce priceless results in output.

But that's why it is important to begin with a careful plan—a course of action—to reach the right customers or clientele, create the attitude desired, and transfer the right information to get the results you want.

I've seen a lot a communications and marketing plans, and I've written more than a few myself. Any plan has certain elements that are as natural and essential as the legs on a table.

One of the most important plans I ever wrote was when I was in charge of the communications effort in 1987 to commemorate and celebrate the Bicentennial of the signing of the U.S. Constitution. This was a worldwide event that captured the attention of hundreds of millions of people. It meant dealing with the national and foreign news media and working with the prestigious Advertising Council to create a national ad campaign.

But the elements of the plan I wrote to construct the whole communications/publicity/advertising/informational effort were really no different from what a small business would use to plan, say, a new store opening or to lay out a new ad campaign to run in the local newspaper, or promote a new product or service.

I say that because the ingredients are more or less the same. The plan should provide answers to the questions outlined below:

Situation Analysis
What is the situation—where are we now? PR professionals call this is a situation analysis. It could include key facts to be weighed about the market for your products or services, the state of the economy, and other pertinent external and internal factors, including the preferences of potential customers. We'll talk about the important job of identifying and understanding your customers in Chapter 3.

Goals and Objectives
Where do you want to go? In other words, your objectives and goals What specifically do you want to happen?

When I wrote a communications plan for the major communications arm of the forest products industry back in 1980, the objectives were to gain public understanding of people's dependence on wood and paper products, of the renewability of the resource, and of the need for incentives to encourage planting and proper management of the forests. Another objective was to build trust in the forest products industry—that it was operating in the public interest with socially responsible practices.

Your objectives typically are long-term. Goals are more specific parts of an objective and tend to be limited as to time and results.

For you, a goal might be to increase by 20% the number of leads requesting a sales call. Or the announcement and opening of a new branch office within nine months. Or offering a product line to a newly designated market next year.

Strategic Considerations

What challenges do we face to get where we want to go and how will we accomplish it? These are strategic considerations.

For the companies in the forest products industry, the overriding concern then was the need to ensure long-range timber supply to meet future demands. So the strategy was to focus on communications to support increased productivity. We had to convince the right people that unless more wood could be grown and harvested, inflationary shortages would result.

For you, the strategy may involve selecting a new ad agency, developing a new catalog, or hiring outside public relations counsel, depending on what your objectives and goals are.

Other questions to answer relate to time and budget and messages:

These are questions relating to goals within the general objective of impressing your customers—specific programs, actions, and events.

Time, Cost, and Theme

The particulars: How long will it take? How much will it cost? Who will do it? What materials will be used? What will be the theme and the messages to be communicated?

If all this sounds like a lot of thought and work, or maybe too theoretical or even involves some wheel-spinning, hold on. I have a way to make it easier for you.

Just flip back to Appendix A for a handy little form. You can fill in this sheet and have all in one place a capsule view of a communications plan for any specific project or program.

Appendix A also has condensed versions of two communications plans I wrote for two different organizations, which you might want to look through merely as examples.

If your plans are mainly in your head, rather than on paper, or if you are laying out a plan without having your key people participate, you're asking for trouble. As my friend Bob Levinson, president of Steelcraft Manufacturing Company, once told me, "You can't go it alone. The trick is to spur your people to adopt your goals as their very own and to drive toward those goals with the same zest that you yourself apply."

Bob also pointed out another key factor in planning. He and his finance man both have the same profit objectives. But Bob gets intrigued with a certain piece of equipment or new system. His financial director winces at the price tag.

"He applies a much needed brake to my enthusiasm," Bob confesses.

So, let your key people complement your thinking. They may well bring a different and valuable dimension to the planning process.

Old Samuel Johnson put it well a couple of centuries ago when he said: "No degree of knowledge attainable by man is able to set him above the need of hourly assistance."

Richest Planner

The late Sam Walton was one of America's most successful retailers and richest men. His story is a dramatic example of a planner who relied heavily on his people to help him carry out his plans.

When Walton started his first store he plotted a growth strategy of concentric circles emanating from his home in the little town of Bentonville, Arkansas. He expanded nationwide from that center according to a long-range plan he devised.

Each of the Wal-Mart stores has 30-day, 60-day, and 90-day plans. Walton reportedly would wake up at 3 A.M. every Saturday to go over weekly sales computer printouts looking for new opportunities and ways to update his plans.

Walton also made entrepreneurs of his employees. Profit sharing, incentive bonuses, and stock purchase plans give his people a stake in the success of this $40 billion enterprise. But Walton also shared his plans and the figures on markups, costs, and profits with his employees.

Sam Walton constantly reminded his people, "Everything starts with the customer." And you've got to always exude enthusiasm, always experiment with new ways, and always promote. He also said, "If you can't measure it, you can't manage it."

Key Questions

As a final recommendation on planning, here are a few key questions you will always want to ask yourself when launching any communication/marketing project.

- What is it that I want to happen?
- How can I best get it done?
- Is this the best time?
- Who is most able to do it?
- How will I determine that it worked?

You may think I've left out one of the most important questions, namely: How can I afford it? You can't afford not to do it; and I'll show you later how it can be even more affordable than you may have thought.

But first, let's talk about understanding customers. We'll do this in the following chapter.

Chapter 3

Understanding Your Customers

Have you ever asked a complete stranger to do something for you—and convinced that person that he was doing it for himself?

Most people feel a bit edgy about approaching strangers. You have no idea how they might react.

But to impress current customers and win new ones, you have to reach them. And the more you know about them, the easier it will be to reach them. You reach them, of course, to ask them to do something for you, namely buy from you. But customers should believe it is they themselves who are benefiting the most by doing so.

If you don't have the right information—that is, some insight into your customers—you always will be trying to reach complete strangers.

With any potential customer, you have to overcome four conditions of resistance. And you probably know what they are.

You have to overcome the customer's or client's:

- Lack of trust. You do this by gaining trust through rapport.
- Lack of awareness of need. You overcome this by showing that the customer has specific needs and defining what these needs are.
- Lack of awareness that help exists. You provide the answer to a problem or show a way to help meet the customer's need or objective.
- Sense of being rushed into something. You calm any fears the customer may have that something could go wrong if he buys now.

Like it or not, many a buyer will believe you are not totally trustworthy and what you are selling may well have flaws—until he or she is proven wrong.

Now I'm going to get into some strategies for taking some of the strangeness out of strangers. These strategies deal with face-to-face contact. But the principles are useful no matter how you identify and reach your customers—even if you don't normally deal one-on-one with them.

Some so-called experts say that when you are trying to impress customers, to sell something—whether you are a real estate salesman, a hardware merchant, a stock broker, a chiropractor, candy marketer, a travel agent, or whatever, in direct contact—you should just be natural. Be yourself; supposedly it's more honest and you are more believable.

The problem with that is that you can't depend on being natural, being yourself, and expecting others necessarily to relate, because only roughly 25% of the people are like you.

Four Types of People

Since the time of the Greek philosopher Empedocles, who sorted people into character types similar to air, earth, fire, and water, psychologists and others have been pigeonholing human differences.

Some behavioral experts now say there are four major types

of people, and each type has to be treated differently. There are:
1. The Assertive. These people want to control the thoughts and actions of others. For them, you have to give alternatives; don't make strong recommendations. They need options so that they have control and can do the deciding.
2. The Analytical. They want desperately to be right. Give them all the facts, deluge them with information about benefits.
3. The Expressive. They want recognition, attention. You have to do some ego-stroking, make them feel important. Be enthusiastic, sell pride of ownership.
4. The Amiable. These folks want approval and support. Be supportive, tell them that others have bought and enjoyed, assure them that it's the right thing to do.

Of course, few people are a single, pure type. Most folks are a mix of two or more. But each person tends to have some dominant traits that influence how he buys. And the odds are that you are dealing with many customers who are quite different from you.

If you are trying to impress customers one-on-one, try to identify the behavioral type as early as possible. Or at least try to figure out what type they are not, so as to narrow down how they might react. Then adapt your presentation to the style of the customer. And try to relieve the tension that always exists when anybody is thinking about parting with their money.

What People Buy

You know very well that people don't buy products or services. They buy solutions to problems. So, you have to help them discover their problems, even when they don't realize they have them. This is true whether you are selling face-to-face or whether you are trying to reach your customers more indirectly—through advertising or public relations.

Discovery of problems or needs or objectives is probably the most neglected part of selling. Discovery skills rely on identifying a type of buyer, relating to that type, and asking questions without making the prospective purchasers feel they are being interrogated.

For example: "So I can tell you about what you are most interested in, may I ask you a few questions?" And: "I'm sure you have a good reason for saying that; would you mind telling me what your thinking is?"

Remember that if you do all the talking, you may be selling, but they may not be buying. You gain commitment by letting people tell you their problems. As long as a client or customer is talking, he is telling you how to sell him. In other words, you can "listen" people into buying.

There's something called the 80-20 Rule, which is not a bad one to follow. Let the customer talk 80% of the time, and you hold it to 20%.

People talk at about 125 words per minute. But you can listen at about 300 words per minute. So, you have time to think, in between the sentences, while listening.

What Blocks a Sale

What typically blocks any sale is a lack of trust or an objection on the part of the prospective buyer. If it is a lack of trust, it is rooted in a lack of knowledge of you and/or your company or store, a fear of the unknown, a reluctance to be controlled by you, a lack of credibility or a feeling that the customer's needs are not being met.

You usually can recognize a lack of trust by a reluctance to talk, lack of eye contact, arms folded across the chest.

You have to find out what the real problem is and overcome it, usually by asking questions.

Why Customers Buy

People buy because they believe the salesman understands them; then they become ready to accept the salesman's solution.

Decisions to buy are typically emotional decisions. But the buyer almost always will base the decision on logic in order to defend it.

Your goal is to gain commitment. The ideal is to put clients or customers in a position where they are convinced that they want to buy, feel eager to buy, and know the logical reason to reinforce their emotional decision.

Of course, you must believe that you are selling a solution. And you know as well as I do what makes for a good sales person. It's ego (self-esteem), empathy (a feel for another's feelings), and what you might call a flare for the missionary (desire to help people). Also throw in more than a little bit of patience and persistence.

I'm spending a lot of time on this direct selling and interaction for two very important reasons: First, it is all about fundamental human relations, how people think and feel and act. And, second, because even if you know full well everything I have said here, the people who sell for you may not; so you can pass this guidance along to them in a way that is easy and acceptable.

What's in a Name

A revealing perspective on why customers buy was turned up by the respected Brookings Institution in Washington, D.C. The organization's researchers looked into why the American automobile industry has had so much trouble attracting customers and why it has been in decline for a decade or so. Some analysts have pointed to high production costs, poor reliability, outdated technologies, and gas guzzling tendencies among the reasons.

But Brookings researchers looked hard at consumer loyalty. They said a prime cause of the decline in the industry was deteriorating brand loyalty to American cars through the 1980s and into the 1990s.

Even though American manufacturers have improved the quality and value of their vehicles, brand loyalty is not only "one of the biggest problems the industry faces, it is probably the hardest to correct in the future," the study said.

Meanwhile, Lexus and Infiniti, the luxury models built by Toyota and Nissan, are reinforcing their brand loyalty with service that goes the extra mile for the customers. Lexus, for instance, has reportedly bought back cars from annoyed owners who complained about such relatively trivial details as polishing marks on the paint finish. Lexus has a course in customer relations that all dealership employees must pass.

Infiniti has a customer-satisfaction fund. To qualify to participate, dealers have to send all employees, including even the receptionist, away to an intensive training session in Arizona.

The pulling power of a good name, a name you can trust, is almost impossible to measure. Quaker Oats, for example, is another name for that ancient commodity, oatmeal. In 1980, the company sold an 18-ounce box of this near-monopoly product for an average of 73 cents. In 1991, the box went for $1.73. Over those years, the wholesale price of oats fell by one third. As a result, the retail price is an incredible 3,000% higher than the cost of the raw ingredient.

Who says there isn't profit in brand loyalty and a good name?

Customers interested in a class of products usually can pinpoint the specific needs they want the product to satisfy. Consumers, of course, go to various degrees of information gathering when they plan to buy something.

It helps if you know how much information your customers are likely to gather before making a buying decision and what information sources these customers will use and what will be their relative influence on the buying decision.

Everybody knows you get what you pay for. And I can't resist telling the story of the fellow in a small town who got married. When the ceremony ended, he asked the preacher how much he owed him.

The reverend replied: "In these parts, we don't charge a specific amount for a marriage service. But you, like others, may want to pay according to your bride's beauty."

The new groom stuck his hand in his pocket and pulled out a dollar bill and handed it to the preacher. The reverend then raised the bride's veil, took a look and dug into his own pocket and told the groom, "Here's fifty cents change."

Three Different Publics

Most organizations have to think about three different publics if they are to be successful and beat the competition. The primary public is made up of your customers, clients, employees, and the community or area in which you operate. If the goodwill of any of these primary publics collapses, you are up a creek.

You also face certain secondary publics. They include dealers, suppliers, government agencies and competitors.

Then there's the third public segment. It's composed of associations, clubs, unions, churches, social, and political organizations and cause or advocacy groups. Any of these groups or publics can have considerable impact on other publics and on your customers—new or old.

Because your main target audience is your customers, you should know about their goals, lifestyles, and attitudes. Some businesses need to know also about their customers' income, age, and level of education. You probably know quite a bit about your customers now. In addition, your trade association, and opinion research and marketing outfits can provide answers. If you are in the dark about who your best customers are and just what your market is, one way to find out is to hire a firm that can analyze your situation, do marketing research, and make recommendations.

Some considerable insight into customers in different market segments also will be found in the next chapter—on demograpics.

Biggest Mistakes

One marketing veteran I know, Vincent DeMeo, has come up with what he calls the ten biggest marketing mistakes. The mistakes surely are common and are easily corrected.

Here they are:

l. Not pushing your unique selling proposition—that distinctive element, method, feature, price, or service that sets you apart from the competition. American Express lost out to VISA when it decided to risk the carriage-trade image of its credit cards and sign up the general public. Soon people realized there was no cachet in having an AmEx card and pay higher fees for no real reason.

2. Stopping success—giving up doing what works because you're tired of seeing the same old ads or offerings. But it may not be until next week that a new customer needs what you have to offer, and he just became aware of you. So, don't stop a winning campaign.

3. Misdirecting your ads or promotion—using a shotgun when a rifle approach works best. Nine out of ten businesses run institutional advertising to broad audiences instead of focusing on sure targets.

4. Not testing. Many companies rarely test their ads or promotion efforts. Even the biggest companies sometimes fail to do so. Had Coca Cola adequately tested the market, the company would have found their customers didn't give a hoot about that new formula they offered some years ago.

5. Failure to address customers' needs. Ask them why they buy. Ask, ask, ask. It could be any of the following: convenience, better quality, different looks, higher value, better function, time saving, and anything that makes them feel better and look younger.

6. Failure to identify the customer. Be specific in your offerings and ads. Focus on primary prospects. Know your customer.

7. Failure to educate. Give them reasons to buy. Provide facts, explain benefits. Tell them why they need what you have to offer. An Oregon jewelry store tired of accepting returned merchandise. It figured its sales people weren't educating customers enough about what they were buying. The owners started having employees tell customers who made the product, how it is serviced, what it's made of, what makes it distinctive, how to take care of it, and what it can do for the customer. Merchandise returns went down measurably.

8. Failure to tell customers why. The more believable, reasonable, specific, and convincing you can be, the more chance new customers will deal with you.

9. Not having a "back end." The back end is the reselling to the same customers of added products or services. Some businesses lose money on the initial sale in order to profit on subsequent sales. Most magazine publishers do this with initial subscriptions. But they make it up through renewals.

10. Failing to be easy to do business with. Walk in the customer's shoes. Be easy to find. Go the extra mile to serve, to please, to make the sale inevitable and automatic for the customer. One big city has its municipal employees wearing name tags with their first name to set a friendly tone. Wal-Mart stores do the same thing. You could try that.

A California company, Select Copy Systems, went the extra mile and took its business right to the customers. The company had a motor-home manufacturer build a mobile showroom for its industrial copiers to transport the product to the potential customers' offices. Sales rose an average of 20% a year largely through making it easier for the customer.

You'd think no business manager would be dumb enough to make many of the mistakes listed above. But some people do. They are the ones who are no longer in business.

Chapter 4

Demographics and Your Destiny

It is said that demographics is destiny. Certainly it affects the destiny of your business. So, you do have to understand that demographics—the make-up of the population—is changing. It will tell you what age and income groups might be your best customers. Demographics helps you spot trends in how people live, work, play, and—most importantly—buy.

Smart business people now, for instance, are using the latest Census Bureau reports, polls of shoppers, and focus groups (small groups representative of the public to test reactions to a product, marketing strategy, or advertising campaign) to figure out how to reach various segments of the buying public.

The country is changing all the time. The suburbs are now not only the power base in American politics, they also are where nearly 50% of the people now live and many of them buy. Some 20 of the country's 25 fastest growing "cities" are actually suburbs. Seven of the nation's 10 fastest growing counties are suburban.

Maybe you thought the baby boom was over. Well, more babies were born in 1990 than in any year since 1961—4.2 million. If this rate continues, there will be about as many preschoolers in 1994 as there were in 1960, which was the peak year of the post-World War II baby boom.

Retail giants such as Kmart, Wal-Mart, Sears, and Target Stores have been adjusting their marketing and merchandise to adapt to a buying market that has many distinct segments. In 1990, Kmart began intensive market segmentation studies and breaking out customer clusters by zip code, incomes, and family size.

Demographics is definitely now part of retailing, says David Serow, a demographer and economist at Florida State University. And retailing people are leaning more on their front-line employees to find out what their customers' special needs are. Obviously, you can't be everything to everyone.

Fishbowl of Information

One merchant I heard about devised an inexpensive way to collect data on his customers. He put a big fishbowl near the cash register. On the fishbowl, he put a sign: "Special Prize Drawing in 30 Days." Next to the bowl were forms for customers to fill out and toss in the fishbowl. The form asked for year of birth, address, gender, and other information. The prize, in merchandise, was a cheap way to gather useful data on his customers.

Another cost-saving way to get a handle on your community and its demographics is to simply call your local paper, TV, or radio station and ask for a copy of their reader or audience surveys. The news media survey their customers on a regular basis to collect the demographic data that will impress potential advertisers. The information is there for the asking.

You probably are well aware that minorities are growing in numbers. Hispanics, blacks, and Asians will account for 80% of the nation's population growth during the next 20 years. By the year 2000, blacks will account for 12% of the workforce.

Target stores, wisely, has used Hispanic film actress Rita Moreno in its ad campaigns. The large food chain, Winn-Dixie, makes sure its stores stock the items that fit the neighborhood. In an area with lots of Hispanics, for example, a store will display more Hispanic foods.

Metropolitan Life has nearly 500 insurance sales people who speak Asian languages. About the same number speak Spanish.

The importance of demographics was made apparent to many businesses beginning in the mid-1960s. That was when the so-called "baby bust" occurred. The number of births took a sudden downturn as a result of the birth-control pill and new attitudes about divorce, women in the workforce, and motherhood in general.

Before that, the post-World War II baby boom had generated a seemingly endless market for everything from portable classrooms to starter homes and from diapers to leisure suits.

But by 1965, births had fallen to below 4 million a year. The birth dearth didn't bottom out until 1976. So, markets were shrinking rather than expanding. Competition became ferocious. Business people began turning to demographics to try to find their niche.

Then came the huge bulge of Americans who made up the baby boom, those born between 1946 and 1964. And the era of the free-spending Yuppie was here.

Whither the Yuppie

Many marketing experts, however, now believe the era of the Yuppie is over. A Yuppie, of course, has been defined as a baby boomer with a credit card and a frantic urge to spend. Many Yuppies are now middle-aged. But more importantly, more Yuppies are putting away their credit cards.

At least so says Marissa Piesman, an attorney and co-author of "The Yuppie Handbook." She believes that high-profile, consummate consumer is now "living with less grandiose expectations and accepting limitations" as to what is bought.

Yuppies have found they can acquire only so many portable telephones, VCRs, CD players, exercise machines, personal computers, BMWs, and espresso-cappuccino makers, according to Karen Meredith, founder of the American Association of Boomers.

In 1990, consumers spent at the lowest rate since the recession eight years before, according to the U.S. Commerce Department. And 1991 was probably just as bad. Some experts didn't attribute it solely to the state of the economy. They say fiscal restraint and a new saving attitude on the part of the baby boomers is responsible. Cheap is chic, says Lillian Maresch of Generation Insights, a consulting firm that tracks the mood of Boomers.

Not only have the Boomers taken on a load of debt, they also are saving for their kids' college tuitions and for their own retirement. It's also a fact that there are no longer two paychecks coming into some Yuppie homes. The wife, or sometimes the husband, is now staying home to care for the children.

Whether or not the Yuppies have been the driving force, the fact is Americans did spend and took on mountains of debt in the 1980s. Household credit grew 50% faster than disposable income during that decade. So, some marketing experts are predicting that spending through the '90s will be at a measurably slower pace. When the Boomers do shake loose of any money, much of it will be spent in the home, in the belief of the editor of _American Demographics_ magazine. The home will likely be the center of life with a host of new technologies in addition to computers and securities systems, because this largest group of consumers will be busy raising children rather than frequenting singles bars. They'll be listening more to tax advisers than to rock music. And when they travel, they'll expect the resort to provide nursery care.

Yuppies' Mom and Dad
In the 1990s and beyond, an increasing number of customers for products and services will be the parents of Yuppies—our older Americans. The Census Bureau says more than 53 million people—more than one in five of us—are presently 55 or older.

By the year 2010, 75 million—or more than one in four—will be 55 or over. One in seven will be 65 or older.

What's equally important, people 55 or older control more than half of the discretionary income and 80% of all financial assets of savings and loan associations, according to The Conference Board, the business research organization.

Not to bog you down with more statistics, but you have to see them to understand the impact of this huge chunk of your potential customers.

Trillion Dollar Income

One in four people in the country is at least half a century old. The customers for your goods and services in this market have a combined annual income of close to a trillion dollars. Yes, one thousand billion bucks.

The 50-plus group is larger than at any time in our history. And, of course, it will grow still larger—becoming the dominant consuming group in the U.S.—in the mid-1990s because that's when the first of the wave of baby boomers reaches age 50 and joins the elder population.

The Census Bureau says the net worth of persons over 65 is nearly double that of the rest of the people in the country. Many businesses, of course, already are serving the older-age customer successfully. But many marketing experts say this rich vein of the population is still largely unmined or undermined.

False perceptions, lack of understanding, reliance on stereotypes all have characterized the marketing to older Americans. This has been true even when businesses have realized that older Americans have more disposable income than any other slice of the populace. And they're healthier and more active than any previous older generation.

It seems as if American marketing always has focused on the handsome and beautiful 25 to 30 year olds. Even General Motors in ads has shown Cadillacs being bought by 30 year olds. How many 30 year olds do you know who own a Cadillac? In fact, three times as many of the 55-plus age group buys all kinds of expensive cars as does the young group.

Young and Sexy

Youth and sex, of course, still sells; and I suppose it always will. Certainly Calvin Klein advertisements are replete with nude body parts. And luscious ladies appear in a host of promotional pieces. But software manufacturer Lotus Development Corp. not long ago threw out its marketing brochure that showed a busty gal in a T-shirt. Ford Motor Co. also departed from the customary auto show practice of using lots of lovelies lolling about on their automobiles and smiling seductively. And no wonder. Half the new car buyers now are women.

One reason—impractical as it may be—why so many ads have been filled with young fillies and jocks is because the ad people and marketers of Madison Avenue are young, and it's easier for them to relate to consumers their own age—supposedly the upwardly mobile.

The depiction of the young buck as the big spender is particularly paradoxical when you consider what has happened to this age group economically. The fact is, members of the under-30 group—the baby bust generation—are generally least able to fit the big-spender category.

Although there are, of course, young doctors, lawyers, and computer programmers with money, the median income of families headed by someone under 30 years of age is lower than that of such families in 1973 when measured in inflation-adjusted dollars. Yes, lower.

Even the segment of the under-30 group that's best off, the 14% headed by college graduates, has had only a 16% gain over what similar young-family income was in 1973. And that gain was only because of working wives.

The reason these young families are doing so poorly is because more of the earners are in service jobs which pay less than manufacturing jobs, which have shrunk. And more families are headed by women, who traditionally have made less than men.

As for the senior market, until recently, senior Americans were thought to be mainly candidates for dull clothes and denture adhesives rather than prospects for high fashions and sports cars. But, increasingly, seniors are seen in expensive running shoes by day and in expensive restaurants by night.

It's Many Markets

Being aware of the size, impact, and nature of the senior market, however, is only the beginning. As Robert Menchin says in his book, "The Mature Market," Once you have segmented the men and women who are 50 and over from the rest of the population, "then the segmentation process begins in earnest. For effective marketing, dividing the mature market into meaningful categories within the broad 50-and-over population segment is as important as separating the young and middle-aged from the older consumer."

J. Walter Thompson and N.W. Ayer, two of the biggest ad agencies, came up with their own pigeonholing of the elder market's different segments.

J. Walter Thompson splits this market into four groups: Active Affluents (40% of the segment and the most sought-after), Homemakers, Active Retired, and Disadvantaged and other.

Ayer, a little more colorfully, groups the senior market as: Satisfied Selves (38% of the mature segment), Worried Traditionalists, and Contented Traditionalists.

Obviously, understanding the breadth of interests and lifestyles among the older consumers is the key to winning this group as your customers.

If you divide the mature market into age categories of 50 to 64, 65 to 74, 75 to 84, and 85 and over, consultants in this field say the first group is most concerned with fitness, appearance, and nutrition.

So, supposedly, it is the market for exercise equipment, cosmetics, luxury cars, financial advice, and travel.

For the second group, about half as large in numbers and worth less than half as much in dollars, has the most free time. Their majors concerns are diets, medicines, restaurants, and leisure activities.

The third group, about half the size of the second group and with about half as much dough, is worried about health care and maintaining their independence.

The final, and oldest segment, but the fastest growing, needs health care and support services most—such services as laundry pickup and delivery, house cleaning, and meal preparation.

Just to accommodate the 85-and-over group, demographers say, there will be a demand for approximately one new 100-bed nursing home every single day for the next ten years.

You probably know that the older the age group the more the women outnumber the men. By age 85, there are more than twice as many women as men around.

The U.S. Bureau of Labor Statistics, looking at consumer buying data for both the 55 to 64 and the 65 to 74 age groups, finds that they spend more than the national average on prescriptions, health and life insurance, home maintenance, heating oil, appliances, personal care, and food eaten at home.

Americans who are over 55 buy nearly half of all the decaffeinated coffee sold, a third of all margarine and canned soups and, in fact, about a third of all food eaten in the home.

Seniors spend more than $50 million a year on travel. By 1995, they are expected to spend at least $56 million. They even comprise a third of all travelers to Africa. American-made autos are bought by those over 55 at twice the rate of those in the 18-24 age bracket. But prestige and image in a car means only half as much to the mature buyer as to the youngster, studies show.

Those insights into the mature market, of course, provide an overview. But these are only very broad-brush pictures.

Shaving Off 15 Years

One important fact to remember, however, when you are trying to bring in older people as new customers is that seniors tend to think of themselves as 10 to 15 years younger than their chronological age. Studies have shown this to be the case. So, in ads or other promotional materials, seniors will likely be put off unless they are shown in contemporary settings, and as active and fit.

Modern Maturity magazine, a publication of the American Association of Retired Persons (AARP), believing it has a fix on the feelings of the older citizen, devised guidelines for advertisers suggesting how they can best reach the customer.

"We stress positive messages," say the guidelines, "and decline ads that take negative approaches. For example, the analgesic ads we publish are those that suggest, 'Feel great with...' We regretfully decline those that say, 'I feel terrible— give me an...' We decline ads featuring words such as 'pain, inflammation, suffer, hurt, ache, and flare-up.' We also tend to avoid anatomical graphics dealing with the analgesics or other products."

The magazine also says it tends to "exclude ads which lump older persons into one category—especially ads characterizing older persons as sick, feeble, infirm, deaf or confused."

Seniors tend to be turned off by anything that's labeled "senior" or designed for "old people." Gerber, the baby foods company, learned that not long ago. The company noticed that many elderly buyers were purchasing the company's baby foods. It appeared that they were buying these foods either because of digestive ailments or because the soft foods were easy on the dentures.

So, Gerber brought out a product called "Senior Citizen" with the same easy-to-eat content as its baby food. But the new product bombed. An elderly consumer could take baby food to the check-out counter with impunity, as if it were meant for a grandchild. But to take mushy food branded as "Senior Citizen" through the line was just too embarrassing.

Of course, elderly customers do welcome products that make life easier for them. J.C. Penney developed a line of clothes that uses Velcro, instead of buttons to make dressing easier for those with arthritis.

The Whole Truth

When advertising to the older customer, it's best to tell not only the truth but the whole truth. These are veteran shoppers. They want it all spelled out so they can evaluate it.

As marketer Robert Menchin says, "Whenever possible, back up your promise to seniors with hard facts—the guarantees, the warranties, the official endorsements and the test results....More than any other group, seniors want substance, not glitter. As seasoned shoppers...they recognize quality."

One national marketing firm's studies found a gulf between how older Americans see themselves and how marketers perceived them. It found for example, twice as many mature consumers want to try new products, brands, and technologies as the marketers thought. Five times as many elder consumers spend more in supermarkets now, compared to when they were younger, than what marketers thought. And there was just as high a percentage of older potential car buyers as younger car buyers, while marketers figured a much lower percentage would be interested.

Many firms are realizing they can't count solely on the marketing judgment of young men and women. So, they are adding older people to their marketing teams—often as consultants or part-time employees.

Most marketers know that many older citizens are avid newspaper readers. In fact, the National Council on Aging says 74% of those 55 to 64 read a daily paper and 72% read a weekend newspaper. Only a slightly smaller percentage of the over-65 corps also reads newspapers regularly. So, this is a good medium to attract older customers.

Many businesses think of radio as strictly for the young

audience. And it's true that half the radio listeners are in the 18 to 34 age category. But, little known is the fact that 55% of the 55 to 64 age group and nearly half of the 65-and-over set flick on the radio early in the morning.

Watching for Fat

In recent years, young and old have become more aware of the dangers of cholesterol, fats, and sodium in their diets. But those most worried, of course, are the older eaters.

Until recently, the frozen foods and the TV dinner, treasured by convenience-seeking elders were unfortunately loaded with the big three dangers. But one senior, namely, Charles Harper, chairman of the giant ConAgra food company, had a business as well as personal interest in finding a frozen food that was not only tasty, but safe. His heart attack had kept him away from the dangerous but tasty ingredients that were so plentiful in most frozen foods.

After a number of experiments, the company came up with a mix of flavorings that were both tasty and safe. The Healthy Choice line was born.

Not many businesses have the capacity to create whole new lines to satisfy the needs of a large consumer group. But almost any business can follow the advice that came out of a marketing study at Auburn University and thereby beat the competition:

- Six in ten seniors in the 55 to 64 age group want senior discounts applied to more products and services and they want more than just 10%. It might be worth making less on some items if you become known for your discounts.
- Two in ten of this 55-to-64 set and a fourth of the 65-and-up group want more courtesy and patience from store personnel. Are all your employees eager to please?
- Twenty percent of both age groups said they had a hard time finding products they were seeking in a store. Is your store logically arranged?
- They also complained about having to stand in line too long

at check-out counters. Watch that buildup.
- One in ten found the print on price tags and labels too small or hard to find. Make those numbers big enough for every body to see.
- Clean restroom and a place to sit down also were mentioned frequently by those surveyed. A couple of chairs or a bench is inexpensive, but a Godsend to a weary senior with sciatica.

I might also add that senior customers, like all other customers want a product or service that performs sold to them through promotion and advertising and PR that informs.

Sex Change

A growing number of businesses are finding that women are customers for what were once considered products and services of the man's world.

When Smith & Wesson launched its LadySmith line of guns for women, designed to fit a women's smaller hand, it saw purchases zoom from 5% of the company's sales to 18% in no time. Toyota sold nearly 60% of its cars to women in 1991, compared with only 45% five years earlier. State Farm Insurance markets life insurance to women through _Working Women_ magazine, realizing that 57% of women of typical working age are in the labor force full time. Many of them are household heads and are earning more money than ever before.

Nike, Inc., found out, however, that if you're selling an historically male product, you can't use the same pitch to women. It started with a campaign that cautioned the ladies that they'd have to "stop eating like a pig" if they wanted to stay fit. When it was apparent that this approach lacked a certain amount of finesse, the company changed its tune to a theme that stressed building self-esteem with exercise—wearing, of course, Nike shoes.

Many big companies collect their own data bases. Some companies have been into database marketing for many years. Clarins, the French cosmetics company, for instance, has been recording names, opinions, and traits of its customers for more than 20 years. The company has used its valuable database of customers likes and dislikes to guide its introduction of new products.

But there's plenty of demographic information available for small businesses, as well. The biggest and best source probably is the Bureau of the Census, U.S. Department of Commerce, Data User Service Division/Customer Service, Washington, D.C. 20233.

The Census Bureau tabulates information ranging in scope from the whole country to a city block with all sorts of socioeconomic breakdowns. Your own state also has data centers which provide federal census data and usually have their own tabulations tailored to local needs.

If you are aware of changing demographics, it doesn't necessarily mean you have to acquire a whole new line of products or services. It does mean you may well have to acquire some new attitudes and approaches to win more new customers.

Chapter 5

Gaining the Most from Advertising

In America, we spend about $130 billion a year in advertising. Nearly $60 billion of it is just for local ads in home towns everywhere.

Whether big or small, however, practically every person who advertises has said to himself at one time or another: "I know that half of my advertising budget is wasted. The problem is, I don't know which half."

So, how do you get the most out of your advertising dollars?

I've been involved with several national ad campaigns, and I've worked closely with the prestigious Advertising Council in planning a multi-million dollar ad program. I've also placed local ads for local businesses. And I can tell you, as you probably already have found out, it's not easy to know which way to turn.

Because advertising effectiveness is so difficult to measure, many advertisers just consider it part of the costs of selling and plunge ahead because of advertising's recognized advantages. If you hadn't really thought about what they are, let me list them.

Advertising Pluses

1. Advertising delivers your message to many more potential customers than a sales force can.
2. Advertising is a way to establish identity, familiarity. Instead of a customer thinking: Hmm, I've never heard of that company, the customer thinks: Yeah, I've seen their ads. I know that company.
3. Advertising can introduce new products or services and do so quicker and cheaper and to more people than a sales force can.
4. Advertising turns up new customers and new uses. Some people didn't realize they had a need until they saw your ad. Some people even see new uses for what you are selling that you didn't know existed. One product that's sold to stop squeaks and loosen rusted parts, turned out to have as wide a use as an oil and grease remover. Customer inquiries resulting from advertising sometimes turn up new, unthought-of uses.
5. Advertising is a way to use either a shotgun or a rifle approach—reach broad audiences or a narrow, specific target audience.
6. Advertising is a means for reaching different customers by using slightly different ads to address different wants and offer different benefits and at a certain time that you want to reach those customers.
7. Advertising can be expanded or contracted to meet differing markets or in good times and in bad. It's a lot easier to trim an ad budget than it is to fire one of your sales people.

Speaking of the flexibility of advertising, many businesses do cut back when times are lean. But, here's a tip that a few smart business people have learned: keep the ads flowing in bad times as well as good times. Why? Because when others cut back, your ads stand out more.

Asking Key Questions

If you have a going business, you undoubtedly have asked and answered the basic marketing questions that must precede launching of an ad campaign. These are the questions that should be asked in any planning function:

- What's the situation; where do we fit in?
- What's our goal in sales and in market share?
- What's the best strategy for reaching that goal?
- What will it cost to get there, and how long will it take?

In addition, the specific questions linked to advertising are these:

- What is our message?
- Where should the ads run?
- What results can be expected?

Even if you don't advertise on a regular basis, you need to know something about advertising for those special occasions, such as to publicize an anniversary, to promote a special offer, to inform customers about a new catalog, to involve dealers in a new program, to raise the number of qualified sales leads, and on and on.

Knowing How Much to Spend

One of the toughest decisions you face is knowing how much to spend on advertising. Some people try to spend what their competitors spend. But this doesn't make sense if you have your own specific objectives. It's like wearing somebody else's clothes. They probably won't fit you.

Other advertisers allocate their ad dollars on the basis of a percentage of their sales. But if sales fall off, so would ad spending, just at a time when you may need to promote your operation most.

Still others try to follow the so-called break-even method. The theory here is that at some stage, money spent for advertising reaches a point of diminishing returns. At that point you supposedly have maximum return on your advertising investment. Spending any more is inefficient.

The problem with that method is that it is hard to find the break-even point. And for most small businesses, that point of diminishing return is way out there beyond what most of us can afford anyway.

Probably the best method to decide how much you will spend is based on the realistic goals that you develop for your own operation, considering all your other marketing costs and objectives.

A word of caution, if you're new at this game: Stick your toe in the advertising water first. Test before you leap. Whether you are running ads in publications, airing commercials, or going the direct mail route, test to see what works.

Another tip that many experts advise: the best results usually flow from using a few publications or mailing lists often rather than buying every mailing list offered or letting every space salesman talk you into trying his publication on an occasional basis.

Should You Hire an Agency?

Another big decision is whether to handle your advertising in-house or whether to hire an ad agency. If you are selling a technical product or have frequent changes in product specifications or don't really do much advertising, you might better handle it yourself. Or split the work with an agency. You write the copy and let them place the ads, or vice versa.

If you do go to an ad agency, I urge you to make sure you know who you will be working with, who will handle your account. Typically, an agency will sell a new client by slick presentations made by the agency's top people. Suddenly these impressive folks disappear and you are left with the young and inexperienced junior account person you may have to educate from square one.

Unless your account will represent at least 5% of an agency's business, you may get short-changed when it comes to service and creative talent.

Another piece of advice: First, make sure you know what your message is, communicate it clearly, and stick with it. If you aren't sure about what you want to say and if you keep changing the ad copy throughout the production process, it can be very costly, particularly in the later stages of production. Secondly, be open with the agency. If you aren't frank and revealing—about your business, your resources, your product—the agency can't fully serve you and its people will begin to distrust you.

Before you hire an agency, get them to come up with a campaign strategy and sample "roughs" of recommended ads— even if they make a charge for their time. This is the only way you can test their creativity and see if the chemistry is right, before you lock yourself into a working relationship.

For Powerful Ads

Whether you do the creative or media buying yourself or engage an ad agency to do the job, here is a list of recommendations most experts agree on to raise the selling power of your ads:

- Keep it clear and simple. You have to catch the eye and begin to communicate with the mind in a split second. If your ad doesn't do this, it has failed. Your money is wasted.
- Offer a benefit. Some ads miss the boat by failing to present a service or product that a new customer needs or wants.
- Paint a picture. Be sure your ad—either by illustrations or words—creates a memorable image of what you are selling.
- Be distinctive. All express delivery services offer overnight delivery. But "if you absolutely, positively have to have it" you think of Federal Express.
- Be specific. Don't say "many people" used your service or bought your product last year. Say you had "5,263 satisfied customers."
- Be believable. If it sounds too good to be true, people will be suspicious. In other words, don't put your potential customers on by over promising or you surely will put them off.
- Put yourself in your customer's skin. What do they really want? One dedicated ad agency writer involved in a weight

loss campaign spent time with a bunch of fat people to understand their problem. The result was the successful ad headline: "I got stuck in a church pew before I lost 70 pounds."

■ Feature one sales point. Your ad can cover all the main benefits. But choose one strong point that is the ultimate selling attraction readers or viewers can focus on.

■ Ask for the order. Untold numbers of sales are lost because nobody asked for action to buy. Use the last sentence to ask for buying action now. "Stop by our store and ask for it today."

■ Don't shortchange. Don't be afraid of long advertising copy. Studies have shown that long copy sells as well or better than short copy. One study of 150 corporate ads showed that relatively long copy (300 or more words) drew 13% more readers that did short copy (100 or fewer words). Longer copy also brought more reader awareness and preference. An ad showing dozens of products or reasons for buying, however, would lose other important features, such as focus, unity, and simplicity.

■ Test it. Let an objective person see the ad copy or several ad ideas to see what will fly. Don't use your employees though. They may be afraid to tell you the truth.

■ Make it easy. Use subheads to carry the reader along. Use captions under the illustrations, since everyone reads captions. Use present tense to make the ad copy active.

■ Include a coupon. Coupons, where appropriate, make ordering convenient for the customer. They indicate you really expect a response. They allow you to measure what brings in orders. And they give the reader something he can tear out as a reminder to buy.

Some experts say there are four basic principles of advertising that are based on the four priciples of memory. These are:

1. Repetition. It imprints the message on the mind.

2. Intensity. Is the ad unique, impressive, full of impact?

3. Ingenuity. The creative approach.
4. Association. Connections to what is familiar to the buyer.

Essentials of Layout

Ad copy is crucial. But so is layout. Here are some principles of layout design you should remember for your ads:

- Unity. Your ad should have unity—a togetherness—among the elements of the ad so that the headline, copy, illustration all hang together to make one strong appeal that's easily understood.
- Movement. The ad should steer the customer right through the ad so that the message becomes clear. The human eye is accustomed to starting from the upper left-hand corner and moving down to the lower right-hand corner. This is the natural way of taking in an ad. So, forcing readers to look at arrows or objects elsewhere in an ad is counter to what's easy and automatic for a potential customer.
- Focus. One element—a headline, photo, drawing, symbol, logo—should dominate in every ad. (Speaking of a logo, a good graphic designer can create this important design emblem to give you greater identity.)
- Contrast. Using colors or visuals to gain attention through contrast or by the unexpected can draw potential customers into your advertising. White type on a black background, a fox and a hound lying side by side. If you don't catch the eye, you don't capture the mind.

Deciding on which media to advertise in is probably best done by your ad agency. They have the research capacity and they deal with the media all the time. But occasionally you should see the media reps, or space salespeople—those who sell advertising space. They have a wealth of information on who reads their publications and how readers make their buying decisions.

It is important that the publications you advertise in are consistent with your image and what you are advertising.

Obviously, you wouldn't see a condom ad in the Catholic Digest.

Another tip you can put to use if you advertise in magazines: Don't design your ad so that it is "right-hand page only." Some ads are designed so that they have to run on right-hand pages on the theory that readers tend to devote more attention to right-hand pages. But if your ad is only "right-handed," you would lose the possibility of its being used in a very favorable left-hand position, namely, facing a cover article, which normally begins on the right-hand page.

Another myth is that if your ad runs near a very popular feature, the ad will get as much attention. Wrong. The reader, in his eagerness to read the popular feature, is likely to skip right over nearby ads.

The Broadcasting Choice

Everybody watches television. So, this is a media must, right? Hardly. It all depends on what you're selling and how big your ad budget is. TV is shot-gun approach. Business product advertising and specialized products or services, with a relatively narrow customer base shouldn't be on TV or radio or in mass-circulation publications. The cost per customer doesn't justify it normally. An exception may be if, for instance, you buy a regional ad in a national magazine—one that appears only in the one region or locale where you operate.

Cable TV does offer some bargains, too, however. Many local cable systems have rates as low as $50 for a 30-second spot, depending on the time of airing. And such cable operators as CNN or ESPN, with huge national audiences, could reach many customers, depending on your product and market area.

Local radio also can be inexpensive, since production costs are relatively cheap, certainly compared to TV. And radio is not just for drive-time. Some 50% of all working people hear radios at their jobs. At least, so says the Radio Advertising Bureau.

Videotex is a system offered in some cities as an advertising medium. Videotex permits two-way communication—between seller and buyer. A customer can get information and can order something without leaving his home.

The good, old Yellow Pages offer another medium for your ad. For some peculiar reason some businesses advertising locally don't make the most of this medium, even though everybody goes to the Yellow Pages when they really need some product or service.

The telephone companies say the Yellow Pages reach nine out of 10 adults. Consumers refer to them on average three times a week, and 85% of all Yellow Pages references result in the contact of a business.

On the other hand, however, one national company is saving $2.5 million a year formerly spent in Yellow Pages advertising with an interesting new system. The company is Domino's Pizza. It has worked out a deal with AT&T for a toll-free number that allows customers to call this single number anywhere in the United States to get their pizza delivery. A computer routes each call to the nearest Domino's outlet.

Timing is important in advertising, as in all things. If you are in the entertainment-recreation, travel or lodging fields, Fridays might be good days for advertising, when customers are looking for relaxation.

Timeliness also can sell. Hershey Foods, soon after the military was sent to the Persian Gulf in the summer of 1990, came out with a new product called Desert Bar for the troops there. It was concocted so that it wouldn't melt in 100 degree-plus heat.

Advertising can be very costly. Big advertisers spend as much as $800,000 for a 30-second TV spot during a Super Bowl game, even though—according to TV Guide—only 52% of the audience distinctly remembers the commercial.

Eyeing New Patients

Two opthalmologists I know used advertising recently for a rather clever promotion strategy to gain new patients. They advertised free eye examinations for anyone in town on a certain afternoon. That day, their office was swamped.

Everyone got a free eye test. And in a number of cases the screening turned up problems. In each case, the person screened was given a form with the test results. On the back of the form was a listing of the doctors' areas of specialty. Also it was noted that both doctors had served as medical missionaries and "routinely partricipate in health fairs and other community activities designed to benefit the public." Translation: We're good guys; you can trust us.

Many of those whose eyes were tested, immediately made appointments for follow-up checks or treatment, thereby helping to build these eye doctors' patient base significantly.

The most potent motivators to any action, of course, are fear and greed. Some advertisers play on the very fears they are supposed to alleviate. One ad by a hospital shows a woman giving herself a breast examination. The ad copy warns: "This woman just missed the cancer that will kill her." Some say this kind of advertising could boomerang against the medical establishment itself.

When Ads Backfire

Despite the pervasive use of advertising and its near necessity in the whole marketing scheme, advertising can backfire and leave a long-lasting stain on the reputation of a business.

For example, the Volvo advertising that showed one of its cars withstanding the crush of a truck driven over its roof. Remember, it was later exposed that the car had been secretly reinforced for the ad shooting.

General Motors advertised its Cutlass Supreme as being so "fuel efficient." But the Safe Energy Communication Council pointed out that most of GM's other models get better mileage. Besides that, the Center for Auto Safety said GM had wrongly claimed in ads that it "pioneered the air bag."

Another corporate giant, Philip Morris, has been criticized

for its Virginia Slims cigarette ads which implied that its Superslims brand could help keep women smokers thin.

Most advertising can be trusted. But when big, supposedly responsible companies pull stunts like this, the public becomes suspicious of the truthfulness of other ads as well.

Since the era, nearly a century ago, when Lydia Pinkham's Vegetable Compound was promoted as a cure all for most ailments, including cancer, advertising has suffered from a credibility gap in the minds of many.

The average adult in this country is bombarded with 3,000 marketing messages a day, according to Business Week magazine. So, how does a consumer remember what he has seen or heard and where?

The director of advertising services for AT&T said recently with surprising frankness, "One of our real concerns is that we have an inability to stand out."

Market researchers say that viewer retention of TV commercials has dropped radically in recent years. TV commercials have become so prevalent for so long, they are being viewed with increasing indifference.

That's a major reason why such companies as General Motors are now looking more at direct marketing, event sponsoring, and public relations to reach customers.

And all these developments have led me to believe that other means of beating the competition hold as much, or more, promise than advertising. So let's look at these others means in the next chapter.

Chapter 6

Making Public Relations Work

Everybody's doing it.

Everybody, every organization, every business that is dealing with the public is in public relations. Some create good relations—with the public and with customers. Some fail miserably.

This chapter will help you take a sound approach to public relations and, in particular, to that most used vehicle of public relations: publicity, or media relations.

When I said everybody's doing it, I wasn't kidding. Even that most repugnant government agency—the Internal Revenue Service—is into public relations, trying to put a good face on what it does. Go to your local library and you will likely see little cards in conspicuous places. They notify anyone who picks up the card of "FREE helpful IRS Publications." The card also mentions: "IRS speakers available for your organization...Call 1-800-829-1040."

Many years ago, I was asked by the head of public information for the IRS in Washington to tackle a public relations task the agency hoped would help inform the public and bring in a little good will. What the agency asked me to do was to write a brief history of IRS showing how it came about and how it had functioned over the years since its birth. The history book was distributed widely, particularly to educational institutions.

Even the so-called "Queen of Mean," hotel magnate Leona Helmsley, apparently trying to change the public's perception of her, gave the New York chapter of the Alzheimer's Association a big, fat check.

Mrs. Helmsley's image is probably so tarnished by her tax fraud conviction and reputation for meanness to employees that almost any public relations moves she makes are fruitless.

Overcoming Image Flaws

But even those with huge image problems can have some success with the right kind of public relations. Exxon, for example, has had considerable success in informing its customers and the general public of the good works it accomplished in cleaning up the enormous oil spill its tanker created in Alaska's Prince William Sound.

Every Exxon credit card holder received with their bill an attractive little folder. It was a progress report on the Alaska cleanup, reporting on scientists' findings of a robust environmental recovery where the oil had spilled in 1989 that created such international attention and rebuke.

I'm sure you don't have the image of either the tax collector or the "Queen of Mean" or even Exxon. So, chalk one up. But that doesn't mean you don't have to continuously engage in new and fresh public relations activities to beat the competition. And I'm going to tell you how to do this most effectively and at minimal cost in this and following chapters.

First, what is public relations? I like this definition: It's the management function that evaluates public attitudes, identifies the policies and procedures of an individual or an organization with the public interest, and plans and executes a program of actions to earn public understanding and acceptance.

I told you in the last chapter that despite the universal use and commonly held judgment of the value of advertising, public relations can have more potential for you in winning new customers, and at much less cost.

The Power of Publicity

Public relations takes many shapes and can be conducted in many ways. I will get into some of the more subtle aspects later. But first I want to give you some pointers on one of the major forms of public relations—publicity.

Let me give you an example of how publicity can work for you. A young entrepreneur started a specialized newsletter a few years ago. He happens to be the son of Ed Behr, a former colleague of mine when we were both reporters for the *Wall Street Journal*.

Young Mr. Behr placed advertisements in the New Yorker magazine offering subscriptions to his newsletter, "The Art of Eating." His ads brought in 175 subscriptions in 1989. Then responses in 1990 from his ads in that high-priced, classy publication dropped to 150.

But unsolicited publicity brought in more subscriptions than did the ads. Mentions and articles about his newsletter in the *New York Times*, *New England Monthly*, *Vogue* magazine and *Food & Wine* in 1990 generated 200 subscriptions. And this publicity didn't cost him a penny.

Then there's Alan Canfield. The A.J. Canfield Company is a family-owned soft-drink bottler in Chicago. A few years ago, his "Diet Chocolate Fudge" soda had plateaued at 60,000 cases a year. Sales had not grown in 13 years.

Canfield began talking to the press about his company's innovative technology and its high standards, without a whole lot of success. He sent cans of Diet Chocolate Fudge soda to food writers and business editors and radio disc jockeys.

Finally, a Chicago newsman, who happened to be dieting,

mentioned the soda in his syndicated column. He said the drink tasted like "biting into a hot fudge sundae."

That was all it took. Orders poured in from across the country. But Canfield didn't stop there. He had a clever follow up idea. He sent a dark brown felt-tipped pen with fudge-scented ink to a list of media people along with a copy of the syndicated column. More journalists and disc jockeys began mentioning the soda. Result: sales of the soda soared.

These two examples show one of the powers of the press.

Publicity—about you and your organization or business—is not only free and gets widespread attention, it also carries the seal of credibility. Believability and trust is everything in building a reputation and image—and customers.

At this point, you may be saying to yourself: "Sure, free publicity is great. But how do I get it. I'm not making news."

Publicity—Not News?

Please, all publicity is not news. Witness the story of Diet Chocolate Fudge soda—an old product born anew. You don't have to make news to get attention, as long as you are doing something that is interesting to others—the readers, listeners or viewers of the various news media.

There's an old saw to the effect that if dog bites man, that's not news; but if man bites dog, that's news. Although many news stories are of rare and unusual happenings, and of conflict and tragedy, the news media is always on the lookout for the occasional "good news" story or the interesting twist that intrigues people.

You may also be thinking: "But I don't want to appear to be a publicity hound." Fine. But you should never consider yourself a publicity hound when you try to get an informative and favorable story or notice in a newspaper or an interview on radio if you believe in yourself and what you are doing to make a living.

Let's face it, good publicity builds pride and excitement. It is a priceless form of recognition for you, your employees, and your firm or business. And if you had your choice of seeing something good in the news media about you, or instead about one of your competitors, which would you choose?

I'm not saying that good publicity comes easily or automatically, even if you have an interesting story to tell. Remember that most news media organizations are deluged with information. There is never enough space or air time to use all the news and information available to journalists from a host of news sources. There are other barriers, too, which I'll explain in chapter 8, on why the press acts the way it does.

The Publicity Market

There are more than 10,000 publications listed in *Bacon's Publicity Checker, Working Press of the Nation.* Other similar directories cover publications in virtually every possible interest area. There are more than 4,800 commercial radio stations, 4,000 radio, TV and cable talk shows, 5,000 cable systems, and more than 5,000 magazines in the United States.

Almost 100% of the nation's households have one or more TV sets blaring five or more hours a day. Radio hasn't disappeared by a long shot. Believe it or not, there are ten times as many radio stations today as when television came on the scene.

Those publication pages and air times have to be filled. In fact, the government requires radio and TV stations to set aside a certain amount of regular programming that meets the needs of the community.

Your Advantage

You have an advantage over some others who would like to get their names before a broad audience of potential customers. Most people, including even most of those who write, edit, and broadcast the news, have some respect for those who achieve results through dedication and discipline, as I'm sure you have done.

Most local newspapers and radio and TV stations also, particularly those covering business, like local success stories and news of important developments that help the community grow. You should have faith that you can provide an upbeat story if it is about somebody who has done something worthwhile or whose business is having a positive effect on the community.

Remember though that the news media—newspapers, TV, radio, magazines, cable—all have their own goals. Their common aim is to present information of interest to a community or an audience they want to reach and which their advertisers find of value to attract customers.

What interests you most may not fascinate a reporter or editor or program director of a radio or TV station. Clearly, you can't control the media. Not even the President of the United States can do that.

You can, however, interest an editor in a story about your accomplishments. What you do professionally may not be front-page stuff, but it could get attention if you use the right approach.

Plan for Spreading the Word

As with everything else in life, you should have a plan for spreading the word about your business or organization. That's the way public relations and media relations specialists work. You need a strategy and information themes. And, as with advertising, you must choose what outlets you want to carry your message.

Here's a tip: Make a list of what you hope to accomplish over the next year. Each item on your list has the potential to be a local news item. You might want to think over the past year as a guide to your future planning. You probably attended a conference or trade association meeting. You may have given a speech. You might have won an award, or been appointed to some post. You may have had a paper published or gotten a promotion. Similar events could take place in the coming year. Be prepared to tell the world about it, or at least your world or market area.

Think also of what will be new and different or interesting in your business. Office expansion? New location? New contracts?

New product? A new employee training program? An anniversary?

When thinking about or preparing any information for the news media, ask yourself: Who would be interested in what I have to tell? How wide an audience would want to know about it? Is there an angle or aspect to what I have done that would be of particular interest to a specialized publication or special section of the newspaper or specific radio or TV show? And what new customers might be attracted if they see or hear about it?

Every day, most newspapers feature items about business and professional people in your community. Such regular features as "Names in the News" or "People to Watch" appear in practically every paper.

Even a handbook or company brochure, if it has useful information could be the basis of the press release, particularly if it is available to the public free. Useful and free are often enough justification for an editor to use a press release.

Timing is Crucial

Even though all publicity is not news, be aware that any experience or event that has long since happened is not normally considered news. Something that has just happened or is about to take place stands more chance of being covered by the news media. So, think about how you can put a timely "spin" on the story you have to tell.

Good timing for getting a story in the news columns would be, for example, when you have just completed an expansion program or hired a new key employee, or when you are elected an officer of a civic, fraternal, or other organization.

You've heard the expression: names make news. What this really means is that a story about a person is usually more interesting than one about some abstract subject.

If you are on a radio or television program, remember that broadcasting's heart belongs to show business. So, the information you provide should have an element of drama or entertainment value, if possible.

Broadcasters—and listeners and viewers—expect points to be made in a pithy manner. Prepare in advance three or four cogent sentences that make your key points. These are most likely to survive tape editing and get used on the air, if the program is taped for later broadcast. (For more about on-air interviews, see Apendix C.)

If the editor of your local paper is sympathetic to the private enterprise system, he or she may even consider writing an editorial about a really significant achievement or large future project and if it is a convincing example of the competitive enterprise system at work.

I mentioned earlier preparing a press release about some accomplishment. A major tool of the trade for public relations and media relations professionals is the news release, or press release as it is often called. Although it can be for the electronic media as well as the print media.

One successful self-promoter I know of publicized himself and his management consulting business successfully through writing articles and then issuing press releases about his articles.

His name is Jeffrey Davidson. He tells of being invited to speak to a group of consultants on the subject of promoting one's business through speaking and writing. There were 50 people in the audience that evening.

As part of his presentation, he told the group he was going to generate an article before their eyes. Then he asked the group: How many of you would like to be published? All the hands went up. Then he said: How many of you have been published? Some 36 hands were raised.

Next: How many of you are using your published article as a marketing tool? Fourteen people indicated they had.

He explained that he was thereby able to produce an article on the subject of published articles being used for marketing and publicizing oneself, utilizing the statistics he had gathered by surveying his audience. He then also had the makings of a press release about his poll.

If that sounds gimmicky to you, I agree. But the point I want to make is that both speaking and being published not only can enlarge your stature. They can be the fodder for a news release and gain publicity for you.

Please see Appendix B if you aren't sure how to prepare and present a press release. There's also an example of what it should look like.

Just the Facts

There is another tool of the trade that you should think about using, no matter what you are seeking to have appear in the news media to make an impression on new customers. It is called a "fact sheet."

A fact sheet is a concise listing of the facts about your organization or company—who the principals are, what the business does, where is operates, how many employees you have, what your special expertise is, where you're located, and any other important facts relating directly to your business.

The fact sheet usually provides background information that would take so much space it would clutter up a press release. But it is a handy informational tool to leave behind if you see a journalist or to have handy if arranging for a radio or TV interview.

Using Your Knowhow

Whatever you do to earn a living, you have expertise in some field. Therein lies the potential for being interviewed on radio or TV to promote your business.

If you are a stock broker, you can tell what the effect on investments is likely to be in the kind of market that exists today.

If you are a plumber, you could tell an audience about safeguards to take in freezing weather or how much a leaky faucet costs them.

If you manage a department store, you can tell how one can be a successful shopper and when to look for bargains.

If you are a farmer, you can tell about how much feed it takes to bring some farm animal to market size.

You can also interest an editor in an item about your experience or accomplishments or expertise. Suggest an idea to a business columnist, and you might be made part of the content of a column and your business could be mentioned in a favorable way.

My friend Nat Weaver some years ago was a struggling CPA. One day he was interviewed by a business columnist about a new enterprise he started. A story about Nat's business appeared on the front page of the business section. He began to get calls from new customers. His business suddenly took off. But that wasn't all. He kept getting calls from the business page editor long thereafter for his opinion and to get quotes every time there was news about the business Nat was in—setting up IRAs, Individual Retirement Accounts.

The publicity Nat received was worth more than the many thousands of advertising dollars that the same amount of newspaper space would have equaled. He was an authority. He was credible. The news stories helped make him so.

Don't expect a story that may be printed or broadcast about your business—even if it's from a news release sent out by you—to be in your exact words. Most stories in the news media are produced or written on tight deadlines as well as space and time limitations. It is likely that whatever is printed will be condensed and in someone else's words.

You can't control what is printed or broadcast. This is true even if you have friends who are editors or broadcast producers. They can only help provide access or an interested ear. You can control only what you yourself provide to a publisher or broadcaster. It must be clear, interesting, and fresh to the reader, listener, or viewer. That is the acid test for getting publicity.

For best coverage, you must understand how the news media

operate, take the right approach, and have a thorough knowledge of your subject.

Rules of the Road

Here are some important "don'ts" that you should keep firmly in mind in dealing with the news media. If you already know some of them, pass them along to anyone else in your organization who might be dealing with the press. They are important "rules of the road."

When talking with a journalist, *don't* talk about getting "publicity." No reporter or editor likes to think that he is giving someone free publicity. Instead you should refer to the information as a possible story for his readers. That's where the journalist owes his allegiance—to the readers.

Don't forget we live in a visual world. All publications think in terms of pictures and graphics as well as words. You should have available a 4 by 5 inch, or larger, print of yourself, with your name and address and phone number written on the back. It could be used as a "head shot" of you that could run with a story about your business.

Don't put off returning a phone call if it's from a journalist. And make yourself available to answer questions on the reporter's terms and times. You are the beneficiary of good or even neutral publicity; be obliging and open.

Don't be afraid to think big. Maybe the mayor of your town would be interested in some development relating to your business—a new facility, for instance—and could be interested in attending and having his picture taken at the grand opening. A developer I know of attracted hundreds to his model homes by promoting the fact that he would give $5 to the Heart Fund for each visitor who toured the homes. His promotional literature listed both his development and the Heart Fund in the headlines.

Don't meet with news people unless you know your facts. Confusion or misstatements destroy your credibility with the press.

Don't say something is "off the record." That's a big turn-off to a reporter. If you don't want to take the chance of some element of your story being printed, just don't say anything about it. But don't lie. The truth will almost always come out.

Don't throw away the news clips. Keep track of attention you get. You can have a story about you or your business en-larged and put on a styrofoam backing and used for promotion purposes at point of sale.

Don't be shy about seeking coverage. If what you think may make news doesn't cut the mustard, the editor will tell you. But the contact with the journalist may lead to a story on another topic that you never thought of and result in positive publicity and attract many new customers.

Don't call a press conference unless you are sure you have big news, such as announcing a major event that will have a huge impact on the whole community. Let me make a few important points regarding the press conference.

Press Conferences

On the rare occasion that you have really big news to announce, here are a few things to remember:

- Send out word that the press conference will be held and why, where, when, and who will speak and answer questions.
- After sending notice to your list of news media invitees, follow up with phone calls.
- At the conference, have a short formal statement, then open the floor to questions.
- Make sure plenty of press packets, with press release and fact sheet, are available.
- Make sure phones are available for the press at the site of the press conference.
- Prepare to get phone calls after the press conference from some reporter who got there too late or one who is looking for an exclusive angle.

Next I want to let you in on another form of public relations that may be of more value to you in the long run than, say, a campaign of full page, four-color advertisements. So, on to the next chapter.

Chapter 7

Building Credibility

You found in the last chapter, along with the information in Appendix B, a step-by-step guide on how you can get good publicity. In this chapter, I'll tell you about a powerful way to build your image in the eyes of potential customers, while at the same time making you feel good about yourself.

A friend of mine owns a prospering jewelry business. His name is Chet Blackmon. Chet works hard at his business. But he seems to work even harder in the community. He is a member of, and on the board of, 17 different local organizations, ranging from the Lake County Education Foundation to the Leesburg, FL, Chamber of Commerce in his home town.

He spends more than half of his waking hours in one civic or charitable activity or another. What is important is this: He is convinced that at least 90% of his business comes from his contacts in the organizations he serves as an officer or board member.

Chet doesn't even bother to advertise any more.

Another business man I know, Larry Palau, owner and president of Better Business Supply, Inc. found the way to build business in a hurry. Six months after he moved to town, his business had increased from zero to $20,000 in monthly sales and was still rising.

Why? "Three-fourths of it came from my involvement in the local chamber," Larry told me. "I believe in giving something to the community. So I really got active; and this exposure, meeting other business people through putting in voluntary hours has certainly put money in my pocket."

Deregulation Fallout

Here's another example of how community service can build good public relations and new customers. During the 1980s, because of deregulation of the telephone business, most phone companies began to consolidate functions and close some offices. This left customers thinking that their service would be reduced or that a utility might be pulling out of their community.

This was true with the United Telephone System in Florida. A survey taken by that company found that only 28% of the company's customers thought that United was concerned about the community and its affairs.

At the same time, employees of the company also were uneasy about the rapid changes that were taking place under deregulation. Teamwork declined. Production suffered. An employee survey discovered that only 40% of the workers believed that company team spirit was high.

So, in February 1986, the company management faced up to the issue. It organized a network of community volunteers made up of teams of United Telephone employees. The new Community Relations Team program had three goals. First, to increase the company's visibility in the communities served by the company. Second, to increase team spirit and employee morale. Third, to enhance the quality of life in the communities served by the company. This, of course, would redound to the benefit of the company, its image, and profits.

Many forms of public relations were used to ensure the success of the Community Relations Team program. Employees were informed through company publications. A public relations specialist was assigned to each team to advise in techniques for reaching the public. A special quarterly magazine was established to report the accomplishments of the Community Relations Teams.

Company That Cares

Members of the Community Relations Teams all wore distinctive blue T-shirts, and they became quickly recognized in the community. In fact, the "blue shirts" became known throughout the service area as the people who care. In turn, United became known as the company that cares.

People who never had volunteer experience before are now feeding the homeless, working with the handicapped, painting fireplugs, building picnic benches for schools, and performing other good works.

In 1988, with recognition that the illicit drug and alcohol problem was affecting every community, the Community Relations Team program attacked the drug problem with a vengeance.

By mid-1989, a committee of volunteers from each of the 21 Community Relations Teams in the state was formed. The "United Against Drugs" project was launched.

Among the elements and activities of the project were production of a children's anti-drug video, sponsorship of a kickoff breakfast with the state's governor, and 250,000 covers for kids' school books.

The United Against Drugs campaign alone paid for itself many times over in good public relations. For example, it brought: more than 1,000 column inches of coverage in 50 newspapers in the company's service area, more than two dozen radio mentions, coverage on 16 television programs, attendance at public awareness events estimated at 3,600, and favorable comments from community leaders and other businesses regarding United's leadership in the "war against drugs."

I've described the United community relations program at some length because it is an example of making the most of community service as a public relations tool.

Only Takes One

Now you may say that you don't have 4,800 employees and you don't operate in 250 communities as does United Telephone. But that's not the point. You, all by yourself, or with only a few employees, can launch a similar kind of effort.

The main objective is to associate yourself with some endeavor that can be seen by the public—and your potential customers—as being of benefit to the community. You not only can broaden your network of contacts (and likely customers) but you are thus perceived as a person who does good works, a person people can trust and do business with.

Don't think I'm cynical. Even though it happens to be self-serving in building images, people like Chet and Larry and United Telephone's "Blue Shirts" become leaders and workers in civic efforts to help their communities as well as their businesses or professions.

Quite often you can be a proponent for a worthy cause and it can directly help your business at the same time. Example: Allstate Insurance has been campaigning for airbags in cars since 1971.

There is, of course, another fundamental reason for wanting to show yourself in a good light, as altruistic. The reason is that—like it or not—many people think of business as a greedy pursuit. They believe that the almighty dollar, even the fast buck, is the sole motivator of business men and women. That's why it pays to be perceived by the public and your potential customers as more selfless than selfish.

"You have to be careful though," advises Andy Peabody, an old friend, who owns Creative Marine, in Natchez, Miss., a nautical equipment company. He has been active in community affairs in his city. "You never try to take credit for good works.

Keep doing good works quietly and eventually you will be
known for what you do."

Feeding the Hog

It is important to establish your credibility with your own
employees first and foremost. If they don't believe you and
what you're doing, it can backfire and hurt your relations with
customers and reduce your profit potential.

In the worst case scenario, your employees may even "feed
the hog." If you never heard of that expression, let me explain.
Employees who feel uninformed, angry, or alienated often will
take out their frustration secretly in a variety of ways, even by
"feeding the hog."

This term comes from a famous case involving a lumber
mill. Mill owners couldn't understand why profits were shrinking. Finally they learned that dissatisfied mill employees were
misusing the "hog," the machine used to chip lumber scraps into
particleboard. Annoyed workers were tossing good, salable
lumber into the machine. They were feeding the hog and thereby
shrinking profits on finished lumber.

United Telephone, which I described earlier, is one of many
companies that made its employees the backbone of its credibility campaign. The whole company was a team with everyone
pulling in the same direction and building credibility. Your
organization can do the same.

School Ties

Probably no sector of the community or organization in society is
more respected and carries more credibility than an educational
institution. This is true even though the American public educational system has yet to do a satisfactory job in educating most
children.

If you can serve a school in some capacity, and that connection is known, your image automatically will be enhanced. Most
public and private schools have advisory committees on which

parents and other members of the community serve.

Jim Miller, when he was president of his local Chamber of Commerce, also took on the chairmanship of one of the chamber committees, the Education Committee. His motivation? He knew that the education of children—including his two sons—was crucial. But his leadership and participation also gained him added respect in the community and didn't hurt his business as a commercial real estate broker one single bit. Not only his visibility but also his credibility increased.

Another real estate broker got together with a high school economics teacher and sold the teacher and his class on buying a house, fixing it up and selling it. By the time the house was sold, some 200 students, teachers, and business people were involved. They celebrated with a banquet and turned over a $7,000 profit to the school. The publicity helped make the real estate broker a familiar and admired figure in his community.

When I was running an organization that served as the public relations arm of the forest products industry, we enlisted deans of the nation's forestry schools in our efforts to inform the public and Congress that the industry was operating with sound forest management practices. We put on tours of company-owned woodlands and conducted seminars for the deans so they would be fully informed about industry practices when they were instructing new foresters or testifying before Congress on forestry issues. Industry's linkage to the respected educators inevitably lent more respect to the industry.

Even schools themselves, and particularly community colleges know the importance of community relations and attaching themselves to good works and activities the public holds in high regard.

When my wife, Nancy, was supervising the community relations program for Lake-Sumter Community College, she was the staff specialist for a performing arts program, the college's art gallery exhibits, and an "Ambassadors" program enlisting top students for community projects. All efforts were aimed at enhancing the image of the institution in the eyes of the community.

At the same time, business and professional people in the community were quite willing to serve on the college's various advisory groups and boards. Some even teach courses as visiting instructors, not only to serve the institution but also because their connection with a college, even tangential, seemed to give them more stature.

No Questions Guarantees

There's a trend in dealing with customers that _Forbes_ magazine has called "one of the hot marketing gimmicks of the 1990s." Actually it's an old sales tool. But it has been rediscovered by a number of companies, and it also deals with building credibility. It is the satisfaction guarantee.

Xerox, for one, has its "Total Satisfaction Guarantee." This is an iron-clad promise to give any buyer of a Xerox product who isn't satisfied another comparable machine anytime within three years. Hampton Inns lets disgruntled guests have a free night at any inn that's part of the chain. Mannington Resilient Floors, the big vinyl flooring marketer, has a "no questions asked" policy that says it will replace any flooring within a year if the customer isn't happy with it.

Thousands of businesses have similar policies regarding returns or faulty products. Yes, it's a gimmick. But it's one more way to instill trust and win over customers. The customer-is-always-right policy always has been good public relations and a way to beat the competition.

Thinking Green

Everyone, it seems, is an environmentalist these days. Some customers will even pay more money for so-called "green" products. There's even a monthly newsletter, "The Green Consumer Letter," that covers new products, and evaluates companies' claims that they are saving the environment.

Some people are so "green" conscious they buy only un-bleached, recycled toilet paper and re-refined motor oil in their hope to save the environment from pollution.

The world's largest women's hosiery manufacturer, L'eggs Products, Inc. decided it would remove all of its familiar plastic egg containers from the market by 1992 and replace them with environmentally friendly, recyclable cardboard.

Between 1989 and 1990, the number of new products with environmental claims doubled. By the end of 1995, green consumerism, products made with special environment-aiding features, is expected to touch more than half of American homes, according to one marketing company.

In a mailer to its credit card holders, Exxon Co. USA boasted about all it was doing to save the environment. It told of its new motor oil bottles made from recycled plastic that would save more than 300,000 gallons of crude oil each year and reduce two million pounds of throw-away plastic a year. It explained that its gasoline is formulated to reduce evaporation and improve air quality.

McDonald's not long ago flooded its restaurants with folders to explain to its customers about its commitment to the environment, going back to the time when its founder, Ray Kroc would pick up litter in the parking lot of his first McDonald's.

The folder noted that McDonald's as long ago as 1976 commissioned Stanford Research Institute to do an environmental impact study comparing paperboard packaging to polystyrene. It stated that the quick service restaurant industry's packaging accounts for only a tiny fraction of landfill solid waste. And it declared flatly that nowhere in the world does McDonald's buy its beef from rain forest land, thereby saving the destruction of some portion of rain forests that may otherwise be cut for pastures and grazing.

So, many companies are finding that linking themselves with a safe environment is a way to put more "green" in their pockets as well as let customers know they care.

I'll Drink to That

The American brewers and their suppliers have taken an interesting position to build an image of responsibility. Through their trade association, the Beer Institute, the brewers have been financial supporters of Students Against Drunk Driving (SADD), with chapters in high schools all around the country.

The SADD program involves parents as well as students. Through education and peer pressure, it encourages students to battle drunk driving.

The Beer Institute also supports another organization similar to SADD. It is BACCHUS, standing for Boost Alcohol Consciousness Concerning the Health of University Students. The purpose is to promote responsible decisions regarding drinking among college students.

Still another related program is All Star. This effort is aimed at juniors and seniors in high school. It sponsors positive role models to appear before the kids to steer them away from destructive lifestyles and toward positive behavior.

Like the utility companies that publish literature telling you how to save electricity, the beer companies are trading some potential sales of their products to young people for increased good will among the public. No one can knock this responsible effort, particularly at a time when alcoholism among young people has been on the rise.

Enlarging Your Stature

I'm sure you are a member of various local civic organizations such as Rotary or Kiwanis, as well as the Chamber of Commerce. As you know, these groups and clubs are always looking for speakers. You may well have been on the program at one time or another. But when was the last time you offered to speak at a civic organization where you aren't a member? It's another way to build your image before a broader audience, particularly if your main topic is plugging some worthy effort or program.

For instance, you could speak about a local charitable or civic event, or even some regional or national need most people can support. Or you can become the sponsor of a safety drive of some sort as a community service. This way, you are identified with an important, worthwhile, noncommercial effort that is admired.

Speaking and writing tends to enhance one's stature—particularly writing. Maybe people believe what the famous English philosopher Francis Bacon said: "Writing maketh an exact man." Possibly some people believe that those who write and publish must have considerable knowledge and intelligence. That certainly is not always true. But for whatever reason, the person who writes and gets published gains respect and credibility as well as attention.

Because communication skills are so important in drawing new customers, I'm going to pass along some valuable pointers on writing and communicating persuasively to your customers in Chapter 9.

My main argument in this chapter is that building credibility and an image of trustworthiness in your community by serving the community has lots of possible payoffs, including:

- Enhancing your organization's image within your field or industry;
- Improving relations with the banking community
- Acquiring new sources of capital
- Establishing better relations with employees, distributors and suppliers
- Making your business more attractive for a merger or acquisition.

The main and immediate dividends, however, will be to attract new customers, increase customer inquiries and bring your business and its products or services to the attention of more customers.

So, you can do well by doing good.

(In Appendix D, you will find a list of possible projects to give you ideas for activities you and your employees may want to engage in to build an image in your community.)

Chapter 8

Why Does the Press Act That Way?

Rare is the businessman who hasn't asked out loud: "What's the matter with the press. Are they anti-business or something?"

The answer to that is: Yes, they are anti-business—AND something.

In explaining why the news media act the way they do, you should know, first, where I come from. I have been a business journalist. I was a reporter for the Wall Street Journal and, later, the managing editor of *Nation's Business* Magazine. I've edited three books on business management for Doubleday. And currently I write for two newspaper syndicates.

I have been on the other side of the table, as well, because I've been in business and served businesses and industries in public relations and advertising management positions.

I also was with a think tank which had, among its scholars,

people who objectively studied the behavior of journalists.

So, I've been on both the giving and the receiving ends.

Instinctively Antibusiness

Many members of the news media, despite professing objectivity and usually even striving for it, instinctively tend to be anti-business. Part of the reason is that so many journalists are liberal, idealistic, and ignorant of how the enterprise system works. A few are even envious because most business people make so much more money than journalists do.

Young people who are enamored with ideas, rather than facts, tend to be attracted to the news media as a career. The idea-driven journalist often feels that the practical-minded business person doesn't appreciate the ideals and concepts that inspire journalists. They see the businessman as insensitive, maybe a little crass.

The liberalism and idealism have been shown in many ways and have been detailed in scholarly studies. For example, "The Media Elite" laid out what the major news media people were like. This major study found that the American media were run by a very homogeneous group of upper middle-class, northeastern city folk. Most of them said they had no religion, and politically they were way to the left of the general population.

Then in another major study in 1991, "Watching America: What Television Tells Us About Our Lives," published by Prentice-Hall, TV writers, producers, and executives were found to be cut from the same liberal cloth. Even more important, the study also analyzed program content and found that over the past 30 years business people, time and time again, were depicted as ruthless and quite often even criminal characters.

The ignorance among some journalists has been well documented also. Few journalists completely understand the workings of the economy, despite the explosion of new business programs on television and the growth of business coverage in newspapers and magazines.

Finally, there's an unwritten code in journalism. Journalists—at least many of them—believe they must follow this code, which says they should "comfort the afflicted and afflict the comfortable."

Just look what happens every time there's a crisis in the Middle East and American oil companies raise their prices. The news media immediately reports that gasoline prices soar and oil profits surge.

The more sophisticated know that most of the price gain is "inventory profits." These are gains that must be spent right away to replace oil at the higher prices that must be paid when a commodity is scarce. It's basic supply and demand economics.

The suspicious columnists and editorial writers pounce on the companies as unconscionably greedy profiteers. They don't explain that most of the profit (and after all, profit is what companies are in business to produce) goes to the shareholders. And most shareholders are pension funds, mutual funds, and other savers. You'd think that all profits went straight into the pockets of fat, cigar-puffing, money-grubbing capitalists, as they (and you) are sometimes caricatured.

We all have to contend with the fact that the world is increasingly complicated. It is getting almost too complicated for anyone to fully understand what anyone else does and how their operation works.

Motion pictures as well as television habitually portray the businessman as the villain and his company as motivated only by the urge to gouge the customer.

Remember Jane Fonda's "The China Syndrome," the movie that came out after the Three Mile Island nuclear power plant accident?

In the motion picture, the utility executives were shown to be covering up dangers in order to push up their profits and soak the consumer. Absurd. Prices that consumers pay for electricity are regulated according to the utility's rate of return. If it has a bigger profit, its rate of return eventually is lowered.

71

And, of course, in the more recent and highly controversial movie, "JFK," the military-industrial complex—again, business—was among those falsely depicted as being behind the assassination of President Kennedy.

How the "Somethings" Work

So, I've dealt with the antibusiness aspect and why this is a built-in disadvantage to businesses seeking to be seen in a good light by the news media and other forms of communication. Now what about that "or something," when business people ask: Is the press antibusiness or something?

The "something" actually is several things. One is the way the news media has to operate. Because most communications media face continual deadlines, they never have enough time to do a story as well as it should be done, never enough time to get a full explanation from a business or professional person about the details or intricacies of an enterprise and its aims.

When I was a reporter with the *Wall Street Journal* in the paper's Washington bureau many years ago, at one point I was assigned to cover the Interstate Commerce Commission, the Federal Communications Commission, the Civil Aeronautics Board, the Interior Department, the Securities Exchange Commission, and the Post Office—all at once.

I literally was running from one beat to another, poring over filings, hastily reading public affairs releases, trying to nail down officials, taking notes madly—all in the effort to get the news of what these agencies were doing and their impact on business and the economy.

Then, if a big news story was breaking, I had to get to a phone and dictate my story to the office so it could immediately be sent out over the Dow-Jones news wire. At day's end, I had to rush back to the office to bang out more detailed versions of my stories for the next day's *Wall Street Journal*.

Although I had studied economics as well as journalism in college and had had previous experience on other newspapers, I was relatively dumb about business. Not all journalists today are as ignorant as I was or spread as thin. But, with all news people, time is inadequate.

So, time is one "something." Another "something" is space.

Even the _New York Times_, which claims to publish "All the News That's Fit to Print" and whose Sunday editions are almost too heavy to lift, can't publish everything. In fact, one of its editors once told me that each night it throws away for lack of space more than $30,000 worth of "wire" material—stories sent in from its correspondents around the world.

The typical newspaper has a "news hole" that may be only half the size of the paper because the rest of the space is filled with advertisements which, of course, pay for the paper's costs.

But, you may wonder, if a paper can print all the high school sports scores and has space for pages of comics and sometimes silly feature stories, why isn't there enough space to cover important business news?

Blame the Public

The reason business has a hard time getting a good press is largely the readers' and viewers'—in other words the public's—fault. Let me explain:

Just as you acquire information and inventory, then use your resources to produce or market a product or service, so do the news media. They gather information to put out a marketable product. They give the public what it wants. And the public wants what will sell newspapers: blood and guts, scandal, sex, personalities, sports scores, entertainment, what shocks, what's funny, what's different, but certainly not what's boring. On TV is what's entertaining and visual. Much of business news is neither. It's important, but dull by comparison to most other offerings.

Sure, the news media covers important and sometimes "dull" events. And the major papers and news networks—both print and broadcast—give readers and viewers the major happenings. But you don't have to be too intelligent to figure out why "60

Minutes," with its controversy and exposés has been on the air so long and is watched by so many millions more people than are most programs on educational television.

Another "something" that's not as well known is that much of what you read and see on TV has been preplanned if not prepackaged. The way a news organization works is that reporters are assigned to certain stories as well as just turning up news on a beat. A TV evening news show plans what it will broadcast early in the day. Unless there is a dramatic change in events or a catastrophe, the network or station decides what it will cover and what it won't ahead of time to enable the news to be covered, reported, edited, and broadcast.

Even when something is covered, if the story has to be told on TV in 20 or 40 seconds the potential for distortion through brevity is ever present.

Since drama and dire happenings are the meat and potatoes of the news media, sometimes the media gets hungry because there is not enough scandal or bad news to feed the presses. Even when covering a subject that's abstract or of a serious nature, there's a temptation for the reporter to try to "hype" the story to make it more dramatic or interesting.

If a newspaper hypes a story to get more readers, and improve its profits, that's apparently all right. But if a business hikes its price to improve its profits, it's considered greedy. Is that fair? Of course not. But it is reality. And it relates to the final "something." The press has an impression about business that it doesn't put the public's interest first. Caveat Emptor and all that. That image is hard to dislodge from the journalist's mind.

The American press, in effect, functions as a fourth branch of government. But unlike the presidency, the congress, or the courts, the press has no constitutional restraints on its power. As you know, the First Amendment to the Constitution gives the press the enormous power it wields.

Two patterns of news media behavior should be noted. One is that supposedly there are two equally weighed sides to any issue. If a radical environmentalist says you are polluting a stream with your waste water, and you can prove you aren't, the environment activist, even if he can't prove a thing, tends to get equal space in a story.

Second, because of the guarantee of freedom of the press, journalists have the luxury of being irresponsible if they chose to. This is rare. But they do see their role as identifying imperfections and shortcomings and often demanding standards of conduct that neither they nor anyone else can meet.

Why Profits Are Scrutinized

Because of the widespread belief in the press that profit is the sole motivating force that drives any business enterprise—and partly because business itself glorifies and boasts about its profits—the actions of business people are scrutinized even more by the press.

There are pro business publications, of course. _Nation's Business_ Magazine, for example. I wrote many a probusiness, private enterprise editorial and article when I was managing editor of that magazine. And there are thoughtful, useful business publications, such as the _Harvard Business Review_. But they aren't seen by most of your prospective customers.

Because business is looked upon with such a skeptical eye by so much of the news media, when a crisis strikes—when a business runs into trouble—that business often digs itself into an even deeper hole.

You know how important good will is. And you don't want to look bad. So, when trouble comes, there's a natural inclination for you to hide or minimize bad news. That's when you need to know about crisis communication. And at some point in your career, you will face crises in your business. That's why I have included Appendix E, which deals with this important aspect of public relations.

Let's now move on to ways of getting through to customers. It's in the next chapter.

Chapter 9

Getting Through to Customers

I'm sure you've heard of marketing gurus who say that success in making sales hangs on the characteristics of the sales person—his or her innate qualities.

Admittedly there are some "born" salesmen, just as there are "natural" golfers, because they seem to be suited to it and they pick up on the essentials quickly and use them effectively.

For anyone who wants to succeed, it helps if they have a winning personality, are persistent, are knowledgeable, brave, clean, and reverent—or whatever other traits you want to identify with people who can sell. But, as you know, there are all kinds of people who can sell, and sell well.

The key to winning new customers, I believe, is technique more than anything else. There are more "made" salesmen than "born" salesmen.

In other words, it's not so much what you have but how you use it.

This chapter is devoted to techniques of getting through to

customers to win them over.

You will win over only those new customers you can reach and can convince that you have what they need and want. If you want to make the most of your resources and bring in the most profit with least output, you want to get through to those who can best pay for and buy the most of what you are selling. You want the right message for the right customers at the right time.

E. Raymond Corey, who taught for years at the Harvard Business School's Advanced Management Program, used to say that the main concern in developing a marketing strategy is to see that all elements in that strategy fit together and the total strategy focuses on the customer. Your product must be thought of as a package of customer values: the brand name, the services, the relations with suppliers, the product image, the psychological satisfaction the customer gets from owning and using the product.

The Affluent Customer

One of the best marketing books I have read in recent years was "Marketing to the Affluent." It was written by a professor who also had experience based on 15 years of practical research. He found that affluent prospects, customers, clients, tend to be different from other people, besides the fact that they typically work harder and longer hours than most people.

If what you are selling is really high priced, you probably know that only about one in every 4,000 households is in the seven-figure income bracket.

You may not know, however, according to the research:
- Small business proprietors, not corporate executives make up the largest segment of millionaires in America.
- Most of the really rich are self-made.
- Fewer than half are white, Anglo-Saxon Protestants.
- Most don't wear $900 suits or other supposed trappings of wealth.

The common wisdom says you can reach the well-off by

getting lists of owners of expensive foreign cars, or yachts. But one survey found that the most widely owned auto among the rich was the Chevrolet.

The well-to-do, however, do tend to live in homogeneous areas. So, there is a marketing tool that does work. In this case, the right way to target them is through the neighborhood statistics published by the U.S. Census Bureau. Block groups with incomes of over $50,000, for instance, can be selected from Census data and purchased on computer tape for any state.

Whether your natural customers or clients are the wealthy or not, you must develop certain techniques for reaching and influencing them; and you have to learn what these techniques are. You aren't born knowing how to reach your customers.

Winning Guides for the '90s

Marketing consultants I know believe strongly in certain principles for winning new customers in the 1990s. They boil down to these points:

- Know your customers. Talk their language and in terms of their self-interest.
- Offer only your best work, product, service. Make sure your marketing plan is based on that principal.
- Be prepared to change with the times. Stay flexible.
- Design specific offers for each kind of customer.
- Listen carefully to your customers or clients so you can give them what they want.
- Screen your clients. Find your niche. Specialize. Go narrow but deep.
- Use multichannel communications. Only one or two ways won't do it.
- Track your results so you know what works best for you.
- Keep up with new technology. Be ready for electronic communications with people you'll never meet.

What We Often Overlook

One of the most used methods of communication is, oddly enough, often forgotten or neglected when we are trying to get through to a customer or client. It's your own voice.

If it seems as if I'm getting far too basic, bear with me. Someone said the voice is an instrument of the human spirit. It certainly reflects your inner feelings, often without your being aware of it. If you are harried or impatient or discouraged, your tone of voice gives you away to your customers, no matter how positive your actual words may be.

People judge one another by voice more than they realize. And the voice doesn't have to reflect irritability to turn someone off. I know an insurance man who is knowledgeable and sincere and clean cut in appearance. But his condescending tone of voice puts me off every time he opens his smiling mouth. It may be irrational, but I'd never buy insurance or anything else from him.

The Eyes Have It

Equally important, the eyes can make a sale or lose it, especially if you have to deal with a customer group or client committee.

Everyone has heard people say, "I'm fine in a one-on-one situation. But when I get in front of a group, I tend to tense up."

Whether dealing with one or one hundred people, in a sales presentation or when giving a talk, eye-contact control is imperative. When facing another human or a group of people, you face an unpredictable reacting force. They may—in silence—be agreeing, disagreeing, evaluating or—worst of all—not even listening.

Eye-contact control is looking at, and talking directly to, each person. It puts you in charge, say the experts. This not only minimizes any nervousness you may have but it also tends to help you control your mind as well as helping you to size up the impact your presentation is having on a group. If the customers aren't looking at you, chances are they aren't buying.

The first step in putting together any message or presentation, of course, is determining what you will say. Whether you are trying to get through to the customer by speaking, by sales brochure, or by advertisement or commercial, the words are constructed somewhat the same to convey understanding to your audience.

Content—the message you're trying to get through—is, of course, crucial. But the visual aspect is too, and is sometimes forgotten.

Projecting Conviction

Anybody selling anything and trying to get through to a client or customer usually wants to project conviction, enthusiasm and confidence. All three are projected visually as well as vocally.

In a "live" presentation, when you're up front, both vocal and visual factors loom large. Communication scientists say that 85% of all information tucked away in the human brain gets there through the eyes. So, the visual element is crucial to good communications.

Let's say you are making a pitch to a group of managers. You want them to buy an investment program you are offering. To make the most understandable and memorable presentation, you should be using visuals—either charts or slides. They should be large enough to be seen by everyone and clear enough to be grasped immediately.

I was at a meeting recently where a couple of high-priced consultants put on a slide presentation that made them look like boobs. The lettering in the slides was so small and the slides so full of details and jargon nobody could see or understand what they were trying to get across.

The visuals should outline your presentation. They should automatically help you store the key points in your mind so you can move smoothly through your talk, and they will help you focus on the main points and minimize extraneous details.

Use a pointer to show the points you are making on your graphs or charts, or a grease pencil to circle an important figure.

Don't uncover a new chart until you are ready to address that point. If you do, your audience will look at the chart and be distracted from what you are saying.

Don't forget to talk to your audience, not to the visual aids.

And don't pass an exhibit out to your audience to examine. They will miss what you're saying as they examine the exhibit.

One technique you can use with visuals is to leave out a key figure until you reach that point. Then you can dramatically fill in the figure for emphasis at the right point in your talk. Beforehand, you can write the figure lightly in pencil on the chart. Then at the proper moment in your presentation, write over the figures (which you audience can't see) with a magic marker. You will look that much more knowledgeable about your subject as you readily "recall" important data.

Being Persuasive

Now, as to the content, you want to get through to your customers or clients in the most persuasive manner possible. There is an effective order of presentation that will help you greatly. Here it is:

First, an introductory remark to break the ice. You can tell something amusing that's appropriate to the occasion, let your listeners know you appreciate being there, or refer to something the introducer said as a transition to your presentation.

Next, state your purpose clearly and briefly, using a visual aid, of course.

Then, translate your purpose into a specific benefit for those in your audience, indicating why it's important that they listen to what you have to say.

To persuade them, you now have to present evidence. Each piece of evidence or support for your pitch should have a visual aid. As pieces of evidence or support, you can rely on: personal experience, the opinion of experts and authorities, examples, statistics and data, and analogy.

Then you summarize your evidence concisely.

Finally, you conclude by stating the specific action you want your audience to take.

Among the forms of evidence or support for your presentation, personal experience carries the most conviction and weight, say the experts, as you tell vividly what happened and how. Make it come alive again.

How to Answer Questions

Naturally, you are going to get questions after any sales pitch. And you should welcome them because this tells you what interested these potential customers the most or tells you what wasn't clear to them and gives you the opportunity to clarify things. Here's the way to handle questions:

Keep your major point and purpose in mind so you don't get side-tracked or have your objective diluted with extraneous questions.

Repeat each question so everyone knows what it is, maybe stating it in a positive way for you. This also gives you time to think about your answer.

Keep your answer brief and direct it at the whole audience, not just at the questioner.

Rephrase questions in your own words that are unclear or too long.

If you don't know the answer, say so. Don't bluff. Tell them you will try to find out and let them know the answer if they will give you their business card.

For the antagonist in your audience, ask that contentious questioner to be more specific. But be sure to stay cool and rely on your evidence in giving your answer. Then avoid any more conversation or eye contact with this questioner.

If all this presentation advice sounds overly fundamental and obvious, then you should be glad you didn't pay a top consulting company for this kind of training, as I once did. What I have given you are main points the consultants provided in their course. And many a business executive paid a hefty fee to take the course and has put the advice to work.

Is Anyone Listening?

As you know, the most effective communication is two-way. If you want to get through to customers, you also have to listen to what they say, as I pointed out in Chapter 3.

University research has estimated:
- Some 70% of the working day for most people is spent in communicating, and 45% of this typically is spent listening.
- On average, 75% of listening time is faulty; we may be listening, but we aren't really hearing.

But the good news is, we can learn to listen more effectively.

To become an effective listener, you have to control your visual sense. Yes, visual sense. You need to visually concentrate on who's speaking. Otherwise, visual interference will capture your attention, since, as I pointed out earlier, at least 85% of what you take in is through your eyes.

Say you are a jeweler listening to a customer trying to find out just what kind of watch he is looking for. You not only focus on what the customer is saying, you ask questions, rephrase for clarification, to try to get a fix on what he's looking for. At the same time, you are listening between the lines to uncover his underlying objectives and making mental notes.

If you are on the phone, try closing your eyes for greater concentration and to avoid visual distractions.

It's all so simple, but so effective, too.

The Potent Written Word

I've given you a lot on "live" communication: speaking or listening—using your voice, eyes, and ears to your best advantage. But you also communicate through what you write, whether it is the content of a sale presentation, an advertisement in the local paper, a talk to the Rotary Club, a presentation for shareholders, or a report to the United Way Committee.

Writing, like other skills, is a learned art. There are few "born" writers. But, if you follow a few simple rules of the game, lucid writing can pay big dividends for you. I'll tell you what the dividends are. But first, some pointers on how to write clearly and persuasively.

Edward Thompson, the former editor of *Reader's Digest,* set forth as valuable guidelines for clear writing as I have seen anywhere. I'm sure his successor as editor, Ken Gilmore, an old friend of mine, would agree with the advice.

First, outline what you want to say. Otherwise, you won't be able to keep track of points you want to make. Thompson recommends putting each point on a separate 3"x5" card. Then arrange your cards in a sequence that makes sense. Or, for short communications, you can simply list the main ideas on a sheet of paper. Then number them according to a logical order.

Only after you've been writing for many years, do you learn to keep the main points in your head as you pound away on the keys, as most of us professional writers try to do.

Second on Thompson's list is: don't write above your readers. Or above your own level of understanding, I would add. Your purpose is to explain something, to inform, not to try to prove you're smarter than whoever reads what you've written.

Another piece of Thompson's advice—and all writers I know would agree—use familiar words or combinations of words. And avoid jargon of your trade or profession. Example: A scientist wrote, "The biota exhibited a one hundred percent mortality response." He could have said simply: "All the fish died."

Brevity Over Bombast

One of the most important recommendations for effective writing is: keep it brief. Brevity over bombast. Remember, the Lord's Prayer has only 65 words. Lincoln's Gettysburg Address, only 226 words.

When you are writing, there's a temptation to get wordy and ramble, rather than sticking to the point. Look at your outline to stay on track. Instead of writing "at the present time," say "now." Instead of saying "in the event of," write "if." And make those verbs active instead of passive. It usually produces a shorter sentence, as well.

Many writers and speech-makers spice up their efforts with quotes from the famous and the funny. Motion picture producer Sam Goldwyn was notorious for his misspoken remarks. He was the one who said, for example, "people who go to psychiatrists ought to have their heads examined." I remember interviewing him many years ago and he was still dropping "Goldwynisms."

Former Yankee catcher Yogi Berra, who declared, "It ain't over 'til it's over," is often quoted for his originally phrased philosophy. But the humor or pithy sayings need to make a point and help to get your message across.

Finally, I would add: Let the reader "see" what you're talking about by using familiar images. A young student I know of showed he knew how to do this. In one of his writings he likened the effects of an earthquake to "sudden footsteps of a giant" and the crumbling of buildings to "rain slapping against the pavement."

No Laughing Matter

Think before you write. Don't express yourself as do some of the people who fill out accident reports for their insurance company. I'll cite a few examples just for chuckles:

"I was thrown from my car as it left the road," the driver wrote. He then tried unsuccessfully to pinpoint his location by stating: "I was later found in a ditch by some stray cows."

Another driver wrote: "I was on my way to the doctor with rear end trouble when my universal joint gave way causing me to have an accident."

Still another stated: "I had been driving for 40 years when I fell asleep at the wheel...."

Those quotes were lifted from insurance forms filed by drivers who were describing the circumstances of their car accidents. They show that incompetent writing may be good for chuckles. But poor writing really is no laughing matter.

Language and thought are inextricably linked. Writing is thought put to paper. Garbled writing is the result of garbled thinking.

At this point, you may say, "I don't really have to write that much or be creative or persuasive in writing." But I'm going to show you how clear, persuasive writing can help you win new customers.

The Power of Publication

If you write an article and it is accepted in a publication that your potential customers read, you not only give them information about your organization or your purposes, you send another very important message. It is that you have third-party endorsement. The publication's editors think enough of you and what you say to give you space to say it. You automatically have credibility and whatever stature is lent by the publication.

A couple of years ago I helped the co-owner of a large real estate firm write an article for the state's real estate journal. It was quite promotional but was written in a clear style with useful anecdotes. It appeared as the cover article. When it was published, the calls began pouring in to the realtor from all over the state. That one article brought the firm—at a minimum—scores of new customers and referrals and many hundreds of thousands of dollars worth of business.

Do you respect the *Wall Street Journal?* Would you like to see your thoughts expressed in that respected newspaper? It's not impossible. Each year the *Wall Street Journal* gets thousands of letters to the editor. About one in ten reportedly gets published. So, if you write 10 letters to the paper, you have a reasonable chance of getting one of them published. Particularly if you follow the rules I gave you on lucid writing.

Why Letters?

Most publications encourage letters to the editor. Not only do they give the publication feedback, but the letters columns are well read.

Some newspapers even give prizes for interesting letters. One of the papers I write for does this. And letters that respond to or take issue with other letter writers are even more likely to get printed.

I remember when I was managing editor of _Nation's Business_ magazine how we would pore over the letters from readers, hoping each month for fresh ideas, opinions, and information.

You don't have to be the president of General Motors, a member of Congress, or any other bigwig to have a letter to the editor published either. Not long ago a letter was printed in the prestigious _New York Times_. It was a long letter. The writer was a taxicab driver.

If the letter had been an ad in the _Times_, taking up the same amount of space, it would have cost the writer nearly $2,000.

Why write letters to the editor of prestigious, national publications when your customers may all be local? You should, of course, write letters to your local editor. But you also should write to the national newspapers and magazines for these reasons:

When you get that kind of exposure, it is seen by other members of the press. You could then be contacted as a source for other articles.

Some potential customers are bound to see your letter and be impressed. Even if they don't see it in the publication, you can make sure they see it later. You just make copies of your letter, showing where it appeared, and include it in your sales literature.

It all goes back to building image through building trust and credibility—the best way to get through to your customers.

Chapter 10

High Tech and High Results

Until Johann Gutenberg devised his system of separate characters for printing on a press in 1440, virtually everything had to be laboriously handwritten. And most folks couldn't even do that.

Of course, people were communicating—"selling" ideas visually—before that. The earliest known attempt at a visual record goes back 30,000 years to the drawings on the walls of caves. Then came the Persians' cuneiforms, the Egyptians' hieroglyphics, and clay type invented by the Chinese.

But Gutenberg's contribution to communications in 1440 marked the beginning of the Renaissance. It was only through this new ability to print tracts "selling" new ideas that Martin Luther was able to gain widespread attention and support for the religious reform movement in the West and win new "customers" away from the Roman Catholic Church.

Fast forward to the early 1990s. International Business Machines Corp. announces that it has built the world's speediest memory chip. The company says it can send eight billion bits of information a second.

Roughly 28,500 years between wall carvings and movable type. Approximately 550 years between modern printing and eight billion bits per second of information.

Why the history lesson? To show how far and how fast communications technology can move.

High definition TV and holographic memories are in the works. There's now a video camera on a chip. The lens is no bigger than a match head, and a wrist-watch videophone is on the development agenda. Nowadays, hardly anyone says: "I'll mail it to you," It's: "I'll fax it." Instead of a sales brochure or catalog, many businesses have turned to video cassettes to push their products.

Customer Technology

You will be using more and more technology to win new customers. You can count on it. Electronic communications has enabled businesses to reach more customers and bring them closer and at the same time segment markets for better targeting and selling.

Did you know that Time Warner's cable franchises in New York offer 75 channels with programs in 10 different languages from Hebrew to Hindi? And by the end of the decade the plan is to have what the company's executives say will be thousands of channels.

New media are emerging that link existing communications tools together. They are interactive and information rich. Customers will be able to view products or services in different forms, as they themselves choose. Some businesses, maybe yours, will be sending promotional information for customers directly to their computers.

So-called hypermedia technology, such as Apple Computer's Hyper-Card, permits users to develop quickly accurate profiles of customers. Hypermedia technology can make amassing customer files simple and cheaper as well as faster.

Wireless cash registers, made by Symbol Technologies, Inc. can let you take the cash register out on the sidewalk for sidewalk sales. A new-fangled cash register about the size of a big notebook is so portable your sales people can carry it around the store to give a prized customer one-on-one immediate check-out service.

Bar-codes on packages are changing. The striped version is limited in how much information it can contain. New extra-dimensional codes will hold so much information, a shipper can list all the contents of a box with information so that no one has to open the box to find out everything that's inside.

And how about a scanner gun for the warehouse that reads bar-codes 25 feet away for faster and more efficient inventorying? They're available.

Desktop Wonders

You should also know, if you don't already, something about desktop publishing and the wonders of electronic graphic design. It is appropriate for anything in print, such as your annual report, sales catalog, or promotional brochure, not to mention full-color advertisements.

Until recently, the graphic arts industry—those people who design and create the promotional materials before they go to the printer—was split into all manner of tradesmen, technicians, artists, and specialized craftsmen. Some businesses still go through all the time-consuming and expensive steps to get, say, a pamphlet printed or slides made for a marketing presentation.

But more and more businesses are doing work in-house with a so-called desktop publishing operation, or they are turning to those graphic design studios that are at the forefront of technology and have the knowhow and electronic equipment that can save you time and money.

Meanwhile, if you produce some of the steps of publishing in-house, your employees who do this kind of work are having to learn more about software programs and production methods than ever before, as technology rushes ahead at breakneck speed.

The traditional method of turning out, say, a sales brochure, involves a process something like this:

Something Old, Something New

A designer creates a rough layout, showing where the copy (the text) goes and where the illustrations or photographs fit in. Typically, the copy is written first. But sometimes it is written to fit a layout.

You see the rough layout and okay the design concept or ask the designer to make the changes you want. Next, the copy, with type specifications, is sent to a typesetter where the text is set in galleys. Then corrections or changes are made to fit the layout. Type is reset with the changes. Color photos are sent to a color separation house with specifications for cropping or other instructions. Any changes become increasingly expensive.

Galleys of type and color separations come back from outside to the designer to be marked up and returned with changes. Finally, the designer pastes up and positions the art work in page format on what's called a mechanical, which has a tissue overlay on which instructions can be written for the people who prepare the film.

In the film-preparation stage, pages of the brochure are assembled, by the "stripper," who depends mainly on hand-and-eye skills to get things lined up. Then proofs are made by the printer for the designer's, and your, okay.

The final prepress product with changes now is ready to go back to the printer to be put on the press.

With the desktop publishing method, it's a whole new story. Design, typesetting, and layout of the pages can all be done in the same location by one person. A knowledgeable designer can create an electronic "comp" on the computer usually in a fraction of the time spent using traditional methods. If you don't like what's been done, the designer can easily and quickly change things on the computer.

What's called a service bureau takes the designer's electronic input in diskette form and, with expensive, high tech production equipment, outputs color proofs, color separations, or film ready for the press. The modern service bureau has color electronic scanners like traditional separation houses that can "read" photographs, slides, or transparencies and separate them into the four-process colors for printing. Color scanners and black-and-white digitizers enable almost any kind of visual material to be turned into electronic signals. Memory technologies allow millions of bits of data to be stored with immediate access.

Film and proofs can be created to your specifications with a speedy turnaround and at fairly reasonable, if not exactly dirt-cheap, prices. Color electronic prepress systems can take you through all the steps from original copy to—in some cases—the final plate that goes on the printing press. The systems are particularly effective when you have, say, complex catalog pages with multicolor halftones or facing pages with art that crosses over both pages.

You can't be expected to keep up with all this fast-paced technology. But you can seek out a qualified design studio—say, for instance, MediaWorks Design in Arlington, VA. It is among the creative operating studios that have the expertise and equipment to enable you to benefit from modern publishing technology.

Video Press Releases

It is impossible to cover all aspects of communications technology that you may use to win new customers. But I do want to expose you to one development that is coming into wider and wider use and has huge potential for establishing your credibility. It is the video news release.

I have told you about the importance of publicity and the value of timeliness in trying to get your story told by the news media. You should now know about the video news release, or VNR, because it is having explosive growth and you don't have to be one of the Fortune 500 companies to use it.

Using a VNR is similar to issuing a printed news release, except that it's a "made-for-television" product.

VNRs are compared by some to the 30-second political TV spots candidates use at election time to "sell" themselves to the electorate. These political commercials have largely replaced debates and speeches because they can reach more people and shoot a message quickly at the voter as a kind of fast-food for the mind.

Corporations are now employing VNRs in somewhat the same way by furnishing eye-catching, high-impact, and particularly timely material to a broad audience.

The Business Advantage

But businesses have an advantage over politicians. With a political spot, you listen with a skeptical ear because you know it's that candidates's bias you're hearing. With a VNR, the viewer—maybe your customer—sees it as no different from another item on a news broadcast. So, it is seen as objective. Another advantage is that you don't pay to have it aired as you would a TV commercial.

Why, you may ask, would some TV station want to use a video news release from you? And you don't pay a red cent to the station. It boils down to money and budgets. If you can provide a visually attractive and interesting and reasonably timely videotape that readily fits into a daily newscast, that's one less outlay the station has to make from its very limited news-show budget.

The video news release began being used on a small scale in the early 1980s when the overnight delivery services started operating and offered a business person a way to gave a TV station some footage in a timely manner.

But during the first few years, the videotape cassettes would pile up on news directors' desks, and nobody had enough time to view them for possible use.

Enter the Satellite

Then came the satellite. Toward the end of the 1980s, companies and public relations agencies could beam their VNRs up to satellites encircling the globe. TV stations could then "catch" them with their dishes. This still meant a problem for TV news directors. They still had to know what was on the hundreds of channels beaming signals to earth. So, companies sprang up that specialized in notifying stations of what was coming so they could "downlink" whatever material they wanted.

VNR transmissions now total probably 15,000 to 20,000 a year, with the sky filled with prepackaged, free spots that can be whisked onto a local broadcast. Variety magazine calls VNRs "gift-wrapped news."

Nielsen Media Research indicates that 93% of the TV stations have satellite downlinking facilities and most of them are willing to use VNRs if they are professional-looking productions.

To encourage maximum use of a VNR, some companies provide what's called a "B-roll." This is 90 seconds of video visuals taken out of the VNR which allows local news announcers to "voice over" the supplied material, making it appear that the material was locally produced.

If this is beginning to sound rather technical and you wonder if this sophisticated tool of public relations is for you, or if you can even afford it, let me continue.

A video news release is obviously more costly than churning out a regular news release. The production cost can run up to $20,000 or so, and the distribution cost, another $10,000.

But when you compare it to the cost to a 30-second commercial on a network show, the VNR is cheap. And if this PR mechanism is used to promote a whole industry or group of companies, the cost could be reasonable for a cooperating individual business.

Skirting Some Rules

The video news release also gives a business much more

freedom for expressing ideas and appeals than commercials do. The reason is that commercials are restricted by the Federal Trade Commission and subject to standards established by the networks.

This, of course, is not to suggest that you should use VNRs to skirt the law or try to deceive consumers. But liquor distributors, for example, have used VNRs to get around the ban on liquor advertising on the air.

Pharmaceutical companies also have used VNRs to inform the public about drugs whose marketing is very heavily regulated, sometimes over regulated, by the Food and Drug Administration.

Your lawyer can advise you on how and when you can use the VNRs, of course.

A further advantage of the VNR is that there is no requirement that a video news release reveal a business is the source of the information in a video release. And many news producers don't care.

Some businesses even have their VNRs produced by a TV news organization itself—for a price, of course. One news service that acts as the Washington bureau for several hundred television stations, including many ABC affiliates, has a division that produces VNRs and distributes them to client stations. While the news operation is separate from the VNR operation, some of the same people and technical expertise are used for both functions.

The ten most widely used VNRs a year or so ago, according to one analysis, were seen by about 70 million people. Eight of them were produced for corporations, one by a so-called public interest organization, and one by a trade association.

Obviously, most small retailers aren't going to start producing VNRs when their market area or product line may hardly even justify using local TV. But it's not beyond reality for your trade association.

Video news releases, along with some other aspects of public relations and promotion may well be operations that you can't

see yourself getting involved with. You may well have decided
by now that, even though it is essential to know as much about
PR as this manual has provided, you want somebody else to
do it.

You may have concluded that you should hire a public
relations expert to get you the most mileage. Fine. The next
chapter will tell you how to make sure you get what you need in
public relations counsel. And what you have learned by now will
make you that much more qualified to make a wise choice.

Chapter 11

If You Hire PR Help

Although you can be your own best PR person in all the ways I have explained so far, at some point in your growth you may well want to hire help from the outside.

No matter how small your organization is, you may well have an advertising agency creating your ads and/or placing them for you at present. If not, I gave you pointers about engaging an advertising agency in Chapter 5. Now let's talk about public relations counsel.

The first decision is whether to employ a PR professional in-house or go to an outside agency. If you don't think your budget and workload are of sufficient size to justify hiring a fulltime, in-house public relations person, your best bet is probably to seek an outside agency.

Tenors and Baritones

In any case, veterans in the communications business warn, don't expect your advertising agency to take on the public relations function, unless the agency has a separate and experienced PR division. Advertising and PR are both communications operations. They should work in harmony. But one is singing tenor and the other baritone. They have similar but quite different roles.

Whether your hire a person to operate your public relations function in-house or hire an agency outside, you need to be clear in your own mind about your objectives. Remember what's in Chapter 2 about planning and goal setting.

Let's focus on engaging an outside firm. Hiring a PR firm is much like selecting an employee. Think about and write a "job" description for what you want the firm to do for you before you even look into what firm you want to contact.

This "job" description for the firm will likely change to some degree because an agency will come up with ideas, functions, and activities you never thought of. But it is still wise to begin by writing a description of what you want done.

Next, you need to decide what kind of firm will best serve you. All PR firms are not alike, any more than all cars are alike.

There is the large "supermarket" type of agency, with a big staff comprising many talents and areas of expertise. The huge firms aren't interested in small potatoes.

Then there's the specialist firm. It may specialize only in certain industries or product lines or in a narrow functional area, such as investor relations.

You also have firms that may perform a variety of functions, but they restrict their operations to a particular locale. Their clients do business locally or regionally, not nationally.

And you have the small almost one-man-shop, jack-of-all-trades agency. This could be a low-overhead, low-cost counselor. But you probably won't get the breadth of expertise or service a larger, midsize firm could offer.

Most Important Assets

The three key assets you should expect in hiring an outside firm are:

- Creativity—innovative approaches and tools
- Objectivity—seeing with an unbiased eye what you
  may be blind to
- Experience—knowing the territory and what buttons to push

One of the deans of American public relations, Philip Lesly, whose company carries his name, lists a number of added factors to consider in choosing an outside PR firm:

1. Conflict of interest. Although, as Lesly notes, some PR agencies may represent both a trade association and a key member of that association, surely it would be unwise to hire any agency that represents a direct competitor or an opposing point of view. If you create lots of solid waste or smoke in your operation, you probably wouldn't want to hire a PR outfit that represents an ultra-environmentalist group.

2. Firm reputation. For counseling and creative input, the "caliber of mind and the character" of the key people of the agency is important. Also has the firm represented for some time substantial and discriminating clients? And how able is the firm in handling the techniques that get the job done?

3. Formula PR. Be aware of the firm that uses in its solicitation a formula for what it has done for other clients. The outfit may lack imagination and flexibility to tackle your own unique problems.

4. Inflated claims. Be suspicious of the agency that makes big claims about results. Everybody wants results. But, it may indicate too much emphasis on tangible functions rather than breadth of thinking, says Lesly.

5. Spilling the beans. Be wary of the agency that talks too freely about its other clients and what it has done for them. It may be revealing confidences and could suggest the firm might tell tales out of school about your business too.

6. Making a fit. Some PR firms concentrate on soliciting new clients. Other firms focus on servicing present clients. Be careful of the firm that can't seem to retain clients. The most effective PR counselors, Lesly points out, are professionals who concentrate on servicing their clients as the way to build their reputation.

Available Functions
Here are some of the functions a public relations agency can perform for you:

Analyzing your situation and your potential market; helping to plan ways to attract new customers; aiding in developing strategies for reaching new customers; providing fresh ideas and approaches; writing speeches; reviewing your sales material; helping to train your employees in good public relations techniques; collecting customer testimonials; acting as liaison with government agencies; improving relations with the financial community, assisting in warding off takeovers; setting up an exhibit for a trade show; measuring and evaluating the results of your public relations efforts; and preparing press releases and making contacts with the news media.

If you decide you need PR help, you don't have to enter into a lasting marriage with an agency. You can hire them for a special event or specific need: a ground-breaking, a sales contest, to start a company newsletter, or to prepare for a news conference, for instance.

If you do hire an agency for a full range of services, prepare to spend at least $10,000. Few firms will want to sign on for less.

Just as you would do when hiring an employee, check up on the PR firm by talking with past employers. What did the PR agency do for previous clients? What are the agency's strong points? Weak points? Would the previous client hire the agency again?

Where to Find One
How do you find an agency? Look at *O'Dwyer's Directory of Public Relations Firms* in your local library. The directory lists firms by size, geographically, and by area of interest and expertise.

After you have found the name and description of an agency that seems to fit your needs, the next best step is to go see the head of the firm.

"The most important aspect of the relationship with any outside firm is chemistry," advises John Adams, president of John Adams Associates in Washington, D.C. "You should begin by meeting with the chief executive of the agency. Tell him what you expect. Make certain the chemistry is right."

John Adams' advice is sound. He is one of the most talented and experienced pros in the business. I've watched his firm as it has served a broad variety of clients over the past 20 years. His medium-size firm is as good as they come.

Beware that there's a temptation for some PR account executives to lean toward your viewpoint on subjects and agree with your reactions on communications and PR questions. The all-too-agreeable counselor wants to get or keep your business. The real professional will give it to you straight, based on his best judgment and experience.

Try to keep at the front of your mind that what's pleasing to you may not necessarily be the best PR approach. It is the right approach only if it is presented from the viewpoint and orientation of the customer it is intended to reach.

I have an acquaintance who is a prominent author. He has always insisted, as part of his contract with the publisher, that his wife design the covers for his books. His wife is an artist. But that doesn't mean she knows what will sell a book. As a result, my friend's books all have rather weird, ethereal looking covers which, I'm sure, are a turn-off to some potential purchasers.

So, listen to the counsel of experts on what kind of PR will work for you. What will help you win new customers.

On the other hand, if you hire an outside agency, you may begin to lean on them for counsel that goes beyond their area of expertise. And sometimes its is hard to know who to listen to—the outside PR counsel or whoever you trust most for advice inside your own business.

It's like the fellow who was hobbling down the street on crutches when he met an old friend he hadn't seen in a while.

"What happened to you?" asked the friend.

"I was in a car accident six months ago," he replied.

"And you're still on crutches?"

"Well," the fellow replied, "My doctor says I don't need them any more. But my lawyer says to stay on them."

So, be careful to seek out the best advice. It should make sense to you based on your own experience, needs, and knowledge of your business and your customers and if, as I've said, the PR message and approach clearly tells the customer what's in it for him.

And, as John Adams stresses, one of the most vital services an outside agency can provide is a fresh way of looking at your operation and your market.

"No business sees itself objectively," John says. "A good public relations firm can help you win new customers by letting you see yourself in new ways that enable you to position your business most advantageously to win and keep those new customers."

And that really is the ultimate objective of this book: to help you position yourself to win and keep new customers and thereby beat the competition.

Appendix A

PROJECT PLANNING FORM

This is a form which you can reproduce and use for planning purposes for almost any communications/marketing project or activity.

Project (Situation)	Objectives (Purposes)
Strategy (Approaches)	Goals (Results)
Timing (Sequence, priorities)	Costs (Dollars)
Manpower (Who does it)	Theme (Messages)

SAMPLE COMMUNICATION PLANS

Following are condensed versions of two plans. The first one I wrote for the forest products industry a decade ago. The second one I wrote for the Commission on the Bicentennial of the U.S. Constitution. What can be useful to you in looking over these plans is not so much the subject matter, but the format and a sense of what should be included in such plans.

AMERICAN FOREST INSTITUTE PLAN

I. INTRODUCTION

Despite today's economic ills, political uncertainties, and widespread mistrust of society's institutions, an era of new opportunities is now opening up for achieving major forest products industry goals through building a climate of understanding and trust in which the industry can operate profitably and in the public interest.

Our specific objectives are to:
- Increase the productivity of the forests, unencumbered by unreasonable regulations, in order to meet people's demands for wood and paper.
- Ensure reasonable and balanced public policies with respect to environmental regulations, toxics, and people's health.

The AFI communications plan proposes a course of action and a budget to pay for it. The plan includes:
- A situation analysis, including the latest public opinion research findings.
- Critical issues, including major trends affecting communicators.

- AFI goals and philosophy
- Strategic considerations, including new directions
- Theme and key messages
- Operating principles
- Audiences to reach
- Communications elements, and
- AFI resources to do the job

II. SITUATION ANALYSIS

The backdrop against which the AFI communications plan has been drafted involves external developments and happenings within the industry itself.

1. Overall Climate

The world's population will sharply increase, intensifying competing demands on the land for living space, food, energy, and resources—including timber. Already, in this nation of abundant forests, spot timber shortages are appearing.

There is growing news media coverage of the world-wide threat to the forests and potential shortages of wood and paper.

2. Public Opinion

Public opinion findings reveal significant problems and opportunities related to the issue of timber supply and concerns over toxics and people's health. Eighty percent of Americans feel the country is in deep trouble. This pessimism seems rooted in concerns about inflation, economic issues, and energy.

This pessimism has led to a shift in the public's regulatory priorities, weakening to some degree, concern about environmental and regulatory issues.

A new conservatism is emerging with rising antigovernment sentiment and some easing in antibusiness sentiment.

The new conservatism among both the public and government officials seems more pragmatic than ideological. People seem more interested in how well government does what it sets out to do.

Confidence in and the credibility of business are still at low levels, with no increase in the credibility of corporate executives. Only one in ten Americans believes what big business tells him. The public tends to blame institutions for causing problems.

This is not surprising considering the revolution in social values: a rejection of self-denial and a focus on self, accompanied by a psychology of entitlement.

3. Trends

The major trends with ramifications for an industry-wide communications program include: resource shortages, the trend toward decentralization and pluralism, expectations of corporate responsibility, and proliferation of communications.

In an era of resource shortages, the forest products industry is in an enviable position because its resource is renewable. The industry is seen as a good manager of resources and one that minimizes waste and maximizes use of its raw material through recycling.

As for decentralization, what public opinion research identifies as preoccupation with self and local interests, AFI is uniquely equipped to deal with the trend through its decentralized structure and ability to customize communications materials to meet local needs.

There is a serious need to assure a public perception of corporate responsibility at a time when toxics and hazardous wastes are frightening the populace. New communications vehicles, described later, can help demonstrate that responsibility and the industry's proactive concern for public safety.

As for the fourth trend, competing communications, the AFI industry-wide communications organization, serving every region, enables industry to speak with one credible voice having maximum impact.

III. CRITICAL ISSUES

1. Shortages

The public does not tend to see potential shortages as a problem of supply that will affect all Americans, an issue that will require sacrifice solutions. Those concerned about shortages tend to attribute them to not enough recycling.

There is little support for more cutting of trees on federal lands, but support for present levels of cutting in the National Forests. So, although demand for wood and paper is projected to double by the year 2030, the prevailing mood is that shortages are not very likely or of much public concern.

2. Toxics and People's Health

Despite an enhanced sense of industry performance in resource management, concern over potentially hazardous substances has not abated.

IV. GOALS

In the light of all this, AFI's communications goals next year will be to increase understanding among target audiences that America can and must harvest and grow more trees to meet people's wood and paper needs. Health and environmental matters also demand communications attention.

We must gain public understanding of: people's dependence on wood and paper products, the renewability of natural resources, the potential shortage unless more trees are grown now, and the need for incentives to encourage investments in forest management.

V. STRATEGIC CONSIDERATIONS

Considering these goals, AFI must be involved in educating

key audiences on topics ranging from clean air to investment incentives, from worries over expanded wilderness preservation to "overpackaging." But with the bullseye of industry concern being the overriding need to assure long-range timber supply, the AFI's principal communication strategy will focus on this objective.

1. New Opportunities

The focus on timber supply provides a major opportunity for AFI's climate-building communications capability to respond.

First, there is industry's commitment to twin supply goals to meet domestic needs at reasonable costs to consumers and build a positive U.S. balance in international trade in forest products.

Second, the public atmosphere is receptive to encouraging growing a resource that can help reduce inflation, shortages, and waste and become the wood basket of the world.

Third, the need to grow wood is real. The Forest Service calculations and projections are historically accurate. While demand will double by 2030, supply will increase by only 90%.

2. Challenges Ahead

The communications challenge is to:

Inform key audiences that unless we grow more wood, we could have inflationary shortages in the future.

Show how forest management can preserve and enrich the land for growing what's needed.

Convince thought leaders that trees on public lands can be responsibly harvested and regrown.

Encourage market incentives that reward planting, growing, and managing on privately held lands.

VI. Theme and Key Messages

The timber supply issue relates to a complex of economic, political, and social elements. So, simplification is needed to make the subject understandable, and humanizing is needed to give the subject appeal.

A simple and catchy theme is required, around which all those interested in the timber-supply goals can rally. One theme that has been tested by focus groups is: "America Grows on Trees. But we must grow more."

Other themes will be developed and considered in consultation with AFI's advertising agency.

VII. Audiences

Although not all communications messages have the same audiences, AFI's activities have been aimed at these categories:

Opinion leaders, including news media, educators, civic leaders and political activists,

Policymakers, including legislators and regulators,

Industry and its allies, including employees, landowners, and forest recreation users.

VIII. Communication Elements

Traditional AFI communication elements include opinion research, advertising, education, industry information, forest management demonstration (Tree Farm Program), news media relations, regional distribution, and communications services (publishing, audio-visual products).

A budget for the year, and an appendix with background papers, opinion research details, and organization charts and other information also were part of the AFI plan just summarized.

Now the second plan, condensed for illustrative purposes.

COMMISSION ON THE BICENTENNIAL
OF THE U.S. CONSTITUTION

I. INTRODUCTION

Historic events create historic communications opportunities. The Bicentennial of the United States Constitution is such an event, and a communications plan should match the sweeping implications of this event.

The Commission on the Bicentennial of the U.S. Constitution was established, according to the Act that created it, "to promote and coordinate activities to commemorate the bicentennial of the Constitution." Communications is an essential function in both promotion and coordination.

What follows is a communication program for the future—for the life of the Bicentennial Commission. It proposes a course of action for the balance of 1986 and for the years through 1991. This plan includes:

- A situation analysis
- Commission goals and underlying philosophy
- Strategic considerations
- Communication themes and tools
- Audiences
- Resources to accomplish the plan

II. SITUATION ANALYSIS

This analysis involves both external conditions and factors specific to the commission itself.

A. External
The 200th anniversary of our Constitution comes at a time of relative peace and prosperity for the nation. Confidence, faith in America and its traditional values, and a spirit of patriotism is widespread. During the 1980s, nation after nation has turned a

welcome face toward democracy and is seeking those rights guaranteed by our constitution.

At home is the increasingly pervasive influence of communications and a growing competition for the eyes and ears and hearts and minds of Americans.

At the same time, tragically, in the United States, as many as 27 million people are functionally illiterate. Literacy tests have revealed a serious dearth of knowledge of American history, our government, and citizens' rights and responsibilities under the Constitution.

B. Internal

Factors relating to the Bicentennial Commission itself exert a clear influence on the conception and conduct of commission communications.

First, the Bicentennial is time-specific. Although the commemoration, by law, will last from 1987 through 1991, when the anniversary of the Bill of Rights will be recognized, it has certain obvious peaks in terms of attracting most public attention.

Second, the commission's communications are limited by the amount of resources appropriated by Congress, generated by fund raising from private sources, or allocated in personnel. Not until the closing days of the 99th Congress was legislation enacted to permit the commission to accept large donations from individuals and corporations and to market its logo for revenue-producing purposes.

Third, while arrangements for Advertising Council support of the Bicentennial have been made, a lack of agreement on what concepts were best to pursue have delayed creation of a concrete advertising recommendation.

Fourth, the nature of what is to be communicated—while crucially important—is complex and abstract. Heart disease or the deteriorating condition of the Statue of Liberty in 1983, for example, are causes that put people or symbols in jeopardy. The Constitution, on the other hand, is alive and well. Although

wise statesmen warn that we must understand and guard our
Constitution lest we lose it, that threat is less tangible: immediate danger is not apparent.

Fifth, the staff of the commission assigned to the communications functions is capable but small and new to the commission.

Sixth, the communications decision-making function is
multidimensional. Strong opinions regarding communications
exist among commissioners. The Media Advisory Committee
of the commission is assigned responsibilities for communications policy. In addition, a new communications advisory unit
composed of heads of professional communications organizations representing print, cable, and broadcasting media industries, also has been formed to encourage media efforts nationwide.

Seventh, communications, in its broadest sense, is conducted by the commission staff divisions, as well as by commissioners themselves, to a range of audiences using a wide
number of themes and means and with imperfect coordination.

III. COMMISSION GOALS AND PHILOSOPHY

The commission goals are laid out in the enabling act.
Additionally, however, the commission has been charged to
give due considerations to:

The historical setting in which the Constitution was developed and ratified, the contributions of diverse ethnic and racial
groups, the relationship of the three branches of government,
the importance of citizenship education, the achievements of
participants of the constitutional convention of 1787, the
diverse legal views regarding the Constitution, reflection upon
scholarly views of the Constitution, provisions of the Constitution, its impact on American life, curricula to educate students
on all levels of learning, and the significance to other nations.

The commission chairman, Chief Justice Warren E. Burger,

has given a more precise definition to the goals of the event: "to provide a history and civics lesson for all of us."

IV. STRATEGIC CONSIDERATIONS

Considering the goals and philosophy of the commission, the communications strategy must involve the education of a host of audiences on a variety of topics related to our history and governing document.

The commission's diverse membership encourages a breadth of ideas for achieving commission goals. So, too, will local interest spur local communications about commemorative activities. Local enthusiasm can multiply the communications resources across the nation. But this requires coordination and cooperation in order to maximize the informational and educational objectives of the communications plan. Local pride, however, can be a two-edged sword. The commission must be even-handed to avoid competition that could breed jealousies and conflicts.

The time-specific nature of the celebrations calls for particular flexibility, localization and expansion of communications efforts as appropriate to times and particulars of events. A number of different communications tools and techniques will be required.

Because the commission has the responsibility of conducting a history and civics lesson for all, its communications must be historically accurate and balanced.

To capture the interest of the public in a document that most Americans have never read, the communications approaches must be imaginative and must appeal to the emotions in order to reach the mass of people and make the Constitution as familiar as the figure of Uncle Sam.

Communications also must take advantage of communications industry trends, such as satellite "feeds," not only to foreign lands, but more importantly from the many Washington bureaus of non-network stations in the United States, many of which are in major markets.

The most effective communication always has been that which has some appeal to an individual's self-interest: "What's in it for me?" A sense of personal pride can stir both the mind and the heart. It can be instilled in many Americans.

Finally, all modern communications techniques and tools should be used in a focused and cost-effective fashion.

V. COMMUNICATIONS THEMES AND TOOLS

Our Constitution enunciates our most precious precepts of governance—the principles of liberty, responsibility, and equality before the law—and articulates the powers and limitations of government.

The U. S. Constitution is the symbol of democracy for the world. The preservation of our constitutional principles and guarantees depends on public understanding and respect for their origins and meaning.

Those are the primary themes that must be communicated to Americans during this bicentennial period.

I won't go on. This gives you a sense of the organization and content of the plan. Your own communications plan will follow a similar pattern.

Appendix B

HOW TO PREPARE NEWS RELEASES

In choosing the topic for a news release, you should remember that it has the best chance of being printed if it is interesting or useful to the readers of the publication. So, the "copy"—that is the written message—should be localized and, if possible, should indicate some reader benefit or matter of interest or concern to the reader.

The release should be succinct, should use clear, simple language—no jargon—and should answer the five "Ws": Who, What, Where, When, and Why.

It should be typed, double-spaced, on one side of the paper. At the top of the release should be your name (or the name of the person handling public relations for you) and phone number and a time for release. For example: "For release after 3 p.m., July 4" or "For Immediate Release" if there is no specific time factor involved and it can be published any time after it's received by a publication.

If the wording of the release sounds too commercial or promotional, too self-serving, it probably won't get used.

Think about trying to tie the message in your release to some major current event, if possible, or to some worthy cause.

An imaginative turn of phrase, a provocative thought, or a little known fact can catch an editor's eye and improve the prospect of its being published or broadcast.

Making Contacts

Outlets for your news release include not only the major local newspaper but also wire services (such as the Associated Press), suburban dailies and weeklies, radio and TV stations, and cable outlets. Not only the city editor, but the features editor, business columnists, and talk show hosts may be interested, depending on the subject matter.

You don't have to have a front-page scoop or a professionally written press release in hand to get acquainted with your local news media people. You should know who covers what. A call to the publication switchboard can likely tell you.

When calling on a newspaper or broadcasting station, phone ahead for an appointment to avoid deadline times. Few places are more hectic than a newsroom at deadline. Unexpected visitors are not warmly welcomed.

Visit the weekly paper the day after the paper comes out to get something in the next issue. For a morning daily, the best time is likely to be late in the morning or early afternoon. For afternoon dailies, your visit should be in the afternoon, after the final edition has gone to press, and when the business of preparing for the next day begins.

For radio and TV, the heaviest traffic periods are usually between 6 A.M. and 9 A.M. and between 4 P.M. and 6 P.M. But the news, program, or community affairs director will know when the best time will be to see you.

If you phone a journalist, you need to be able to state the essence of your story in a few words to arouse interest. But it is better to present the release in person if possible.

The reasons you should try to see the journalist in person are:

First, if the journalist is willing to take the time to see you, this indicates he or she sees the possibility of a story. Second, if the journalist sits down to talk with you, looks at the release you provide, and asks questions, he feels he has an investment of precious time and will want to make the most of it. Finally, you probably can be more convincing and appealing face-to-face. You establish rapport. It could lead to future stories. You could even become a regular source and be quoted in other stories relating to your business.

If you are going to make an important talk somewhere, this can be the topic for a brief release or "memo to editors" telling when and where it will be. Then after the speech, another release about what you said.

Topics for news releases could include: awards, honors, civic activities, writings, new products, office expansion or relocation, service offerings, new contracts, bids and awards, research results, survey findings, anniversaries, projected plans, joint ventures, trends, projections, association memberships, appointments, lower costs, seminars attended, grand openings.

SAMPLE NEWS RELEASE

For Immediate Release

For more information:
Contact: Joseph Merchant
Owner, ABC Parts, Inc.
321-4567

Merchant to Address Marketing Meeting

Joseph Merchant, who owns Cityville's largest auto parts outlet, will speak before the Smith County Marketing Association's monthly meeting at Noon, Thursday, Feb. 7.

The topic of his talk will be "Marketing's Nine Biggest Blunders."

Merchant has owned ABC Parts, Inc. for the past 6 years. He came here from Townburg, where he was parts manager for Rathbun Auto Services.

ABC Parts, Inc., last May won the Cityville Chamber of Commerce business-of-the-month recognition award.

Merchant is vice president of Cityville Rotary Club. He has been active in the Memorial Hospital Fund Drive and is division chairman of the Heart Association.

The local businessman has a B.S. degree in marketing from Penn State, where he played varsity basketball.

"Nobody's perfect," Merchant said, "But many of us make marketing blunders that we could avoid with a little foresight. I have found nine mistakes to be most prevalent. And I'll pass them along in this talk."

\#

Appendix C

YOU'RE ON THE AIR

Here are tips if you appear on radio or television to make your business better known and win new customers:

If you want to get on radio or TV, see the program director in smaller towns and the public affairs director in larger cities. On a talk show or combination news-talk show, see the producer, who books the people appearing on the show.

Radio and TV interviews seem to be spontaneous, unrehearsed events. Questions and answers appear, and generally are, off-the-cuff. Certainly there's no script. But that doesn't mean you shouldn't rehearse and be thoroughly prepared when you are to go on a radio or TV talk show to promote yourself and your business.

First, figure out in advance the most important points you want the audience to hear and understand. Remember, nobody out there listening or watching will be interested unless what you say seems to affect them in some fashion. Limit your message to two or three main points. That's all anybody will remember and probably all you can say in the time you will have. Try to work in these points no matter what specific questions are asked. Speak clearly and sincerely.

Second, before your appearance, make sure the interviewer—the host of the show—has information in hand about you and your business.

You also could suggest question areas for the host. Many of them appreciate knowing what you feel most comfortable talking about.

Tough Question Rehearsal
Before you go on the show, have someone help you by asking you a set of tough questions that conceivably might get asked on the air. When you respond to rehearsal questions,

record your answers—either on audio or video—to see how you
sound and if your answers are clear, informative, and persuasive.

Try to think of some examples or figures or other evidence
that backs up and reinforces the points you want to make on
the air.

Find out who the audience is likely to be at the time you are
interviewed. Then imagine you are talking to one of them once
you are on the show.

When you are on the air, be open and friendly as you would
be in any lively conversation. Avoid any argument. But respond
pleasantly with correct information if the interviewer has his
facts wrong.

If you get a loaded question, try to turn it around. If the
interviewer asks, for instance, "Why do you and other similar
businesses continue to pollute the air with fumes from your
operations?" You could respond: "Apparently you are not
familiar with all the steps we have taken to create a more healthy
environment."

Maintain eye contact with your interviewer or on another
guest, when that guest is talking. Don't let your eyes roam
around the studio or look down when you speak. To make a key
point, look smack into the camera and at the viewers. That's the
camera with the red light.

Avoid the heavy beard, the wild tie, or plunging neckline,
whatever the case may be. They're distracting. Don't wear
anything flashy or shiny that could reflect the studio lights.
Avoid extremely light or dark clothing.

Try not to clench your fists, fold your arms, or otherwise
look as if you are on the defensive. Try to seem relaxed, even
if you aren't.

Appendix D

COMMUNITY PROJECTS

Here are samples of community projects you may want to consider to enhance your image and that of your business in your community:

1. Sponsor with your county health unit a seminar on prenatal and postnatal care.

2. Offer donations of your business's products or services to a cultural organization's outing.

3. Speak at a school's "Career Day" to inform students about your line of work.

4. Volunteer to sell tickets at a civic organization's air show.

5. Sponsor and speak at a March of Dimes luncheon.

6. Invite and introduce a drug abuse expert for your children's school Parent-Teachers meeting.

7. Set up a scholarship program at the community college for the local high school graduates.

8. Put on a swim meet for inner-city youngsters.

9. Host a hot dog lunch and fund-raiser to send at-risk kids to camp.

10. Start a drive to build a new day care center.

Appendix E

WHEN THINGS GO WRONG

Murphy's Law dictates that inevitably something sometime will go wrong in your business.

It may involve your credit, your employees, your relations with local or state government, a law suit, a code change, a fire. You may well be faultless. Or you may have goofed.

If it affects the public in any way, you can be sure you will be on the spot to shoulder the blame. You will want to preserve your reputation and make sure your customers or clients aren't turned off. You can't afford to have a bad press.

Your first instinct may be to cover up. That was Richard Nixon's first instinct, too. And you know what the Watergate scandal led to.

If your business comes under scrutiny by a public agency or by the news media, here is what the best public relations counselors advise:

1. Be accessible, above board, and honest. This goes for your employees as well as for those outside of your business. Employees need to know what is going on and feel they're on the team. Remember when the Challenger space shuttle exploded in 1986? The Morton Thiokol company was blamed for faulty equipment which made the booster rocket malfunction. As if this publicity wasn't bad enough, a company engineer claimed that he had warned management about the faulty part but that his warnings had been ignored. This really put the company on the griddle. So, good PR begins at home.

2. As soon as you know you have a problem, bring together all those concerned to figure out the best strategy for solving the problem and so everyone concerned will be playing from the same sheet of music, so to speak, when you communicate with a government agency or the press.

3. Have one person as the spokesman—you, or a key and

knowledgeable employee if he or she is loyal, informed, confident, and can gain trust from the press.

4. Give the press what it wants to know if humanly possible. Withholding information or letting go piece by piece of what happened or what is being done only prolongs the agony and makes for more stories and the prospect of further bad publicity.

5. Stay cool. Don't get emotional. A calm posture will be more reassuring to all.

6. Be prepared to begin with. This can be done in two ways. First, you should have developed credibility with the press over the years so that you know them and they know you. Second, have a plan for emergencies so that you know who will do what and when, if the worst happens.

A Specific Crisis Plan

One of the best crisis communications plans I've seen was put together by James W. Plumb, Washington Public Relations Counselors, Bethesda, MD. Jim and I worked together in industry public relations several years ago. With his okay, I have boiled down the crisis management advice to its essentials. It's for your future use in hopes that you will never need it but that you'll be prepared if you do.

A crisis communications plan is like a fire extinguisher, a life boat, or flood insurance. You should be on guard for two main kinds of crisis: the unexpected, such a fire in your facilities, and the expected, such as passage of some adverse legislation that you may have seen coming for many months but weren't sure just when it would happen or precisely how it would hurt you.

In either expected or unexpected events, even rudimentary preparation can help ward off the worse and could even turn the event into a positive opportunity.

The particulars of the crisis management plan that follows may have elements that you would never use. But you can look it over and pick and choose what fits your situation.

The skill with which Johnson & Johnson handled the Extra-

Strength Tylenol poisonings in 1982 and 1986 was an exemplary case. The company's actions in immediately removing the product and then switching to tamper-proof "caplets" not only calmed the national frenzy, it also ultimately resulted in an increased share of market for the pain-killer.

Laying the Groundwork

Large corporations frequently survey the public to see how they stand with various groups important to them. Public opinion surveys may be beyond your budget. But it's important to have a sense of how your operations are perceived in the community and in your market area.

One way to ensure that your business is seen in a good light is to undertake a community relations program aimed at building your image. Build trust ahead of time, so you have an established reputation and a good working relationship with the community leaders, customers, public officials and the news media. You are likely to get more sympathetic treatment if you are known and well thought of.

Beyond laying the groundwork with good public relations and establishing a good public reputation, you should have a crisis management plan that will work for either expected or unexpected trouble.

Statement Sets Tone

The first step in a crisis management plan is drafting a policy statement. It sets the tone and it lets everyone both inside and outside the company know your position. Here's an example:

"It is our policy in an emergency situation to provide the news media, government and community leaders, and employees with accurate information at the earliest stages of the situation. The information will be based on facts and will have the approval of management. It is essential in an emergency or crisis to maintain honesty, candor, and professional behavior when communicating our position.

"All crisis-related actions and decisions are coordinated through an emergency-management team.

"All employees will assist the crisis-management team in identifying potential emergencies, gathering facts, and bringing emergency situations to a satisfactory conclusion.

"In a crisis or emergency, all employees should refrain from public statements or speculation on an emergency's cause or effects and should refer all requests for comments, statements, interviews, or photographs to the crisis-management team."

The policy statement should be distributed to all in your organization and discussed with those likely to have outside contacts, especially telephone operators and receptionists.

For years, airlines have led the way in crisis management and communications. Typically a single spokesperson makes all statements about an accident or incident, backed by a team of legal, policy, and technical people.

Your spokesperson should probably be you, the top executive, as was the case with Johnson & Johnson.

Cage the Lawyers

Your lawyer probably has to be part of the crisis team. But as *Fortune* magazine once cautioned: "Cage your lawyers. They will always tell you to keep your mouth shut. But in many crisis situations your potential legal liability may be trivial compared with the risk of alienating your customers, employees, or regulators." So, make sure you weigh carefully such lawyerly advise.

All employees should know who makes up the crisis team, including who the spokesperson is.

An information-gathering system should be set up with a log to record all phone calls and complaints so you know who has contacted your operation and when and what they have said.

Threatening Calls

Public threats are one form of emergency. Here are ways to handled a threatening phone call:

a. Don't put the caller on hold or transfer the call unless asked to do so.
b. Start taking notes as soon as you realize the nature of the call.
c. Don't interrupt the caller. Let him finish his statement.
d. Don't try to pretend you aren't alarmed or aren't taking it seriously. Underreacting can be a bad as overreacting.
e. If a threat is made, ask the caller to repeat the threat. Try to get as much specific information as possible, such as when and where something will happen, and what exactly does the caller want. The more that's said, the easier it may be for authorities to identify the caller.

It is always better for employees to hear about an issue or emergency from the employer, rather than hearing rumors or picking up information outside of your business. So, be sure to set up an employee briefing system.

What an Investigator Needs
Information gathering should be led by a key investigator. Here's a checklist for the investigation:
a. Date and time of initial notification.
b. Nature of issue, event, emergency, or complaint.
c. Scope of the event.
d. Possibility of change in scope.
e. Extent of public awareness and media attention.
f. Potential implications for health, legal, political, public relations.
g. How the situation is being alleviated or resolved.

You need allies. Credible allies can support your position. So, list all groups and individuals who could stand with you in a crisis.

Make sure your lists of news media people and government

officials are up to date as well as lists of others you may need to contact in an emergency.

Here are some guidelines for dealing with a crisis, once it comes:

First, determine the company's role. Is it your problem alone, or is it a problem your industry or field has? Should your trade association be involved?

Second, set objectives. The aim of communications should be to quell the flames of controversy and minimize unwarranted fears or concerns, get the story in and out of the news as quickly as possible, and relay needed information to customers, particularly in the event of, say, a product recall or contamination.

Third, develop an interim statement even if all you can say initially is that you are investigating the situation. This at least shows concern on your part.

Fourth, update the statement. Prepare to distribute information once you know what has happened and you have decided how to alleviate the problem. Stick to the statement.

Fifth, Make the facts available as soon as possible even if the news is bad. Don't wait for the news media to drag it out of you. Also don't delay in responding to an unfair charge or attack.

Sixth, always talk to the audience's self-interest. Discuss your position in terms of the community' interests, rather than yours.

Dow Chemical Company, which has weathered its share of crises in recent years, has adopted a "4 C" approach to emergencies: Candor, Concern, Compassion, Cooperation.

Dow believes scientific facts usually are effective in an emergency. When emotions are running high, however, cold scientific facts have relatively little effect. Dow has suggested for crisis briefings:

a. Recognize that a problem exists, even if only in the public mind.
b. Try to provide perspective. It may look bad on the surface but not be truly significant.

   c. Project a "we care" attitude and a sense of urgency in dealing with it.

Briefing the News Media

Here's a press-briefing checklist:

   a. Hold the briefing only when you have sufficient information to pass along.

   b. Make sure the location of the briefing is easily accessible and, if possible, on site.

   c. If it is big news, make sure there are plenty of electrical outlets for television lights.

   d. The spokesperson should have a prepared statement for reading and handing out to reporters. The statement should contain perspective on the situation and what is being done to fix it.

   e. Stick to the subject at hand. Don't get sidetracked. If other matters arise, say you'll be glad to talk about them later.

   f. Have experts or technical people on hand to help you answer technical questions.

   g. If possible, practice the briefing routine with members of your crisis team acting as reporters and asking tough questions.

These are some common press interview techniques that might throw you off but which you can prepare for :

REPORTER: "Are you saying that..."

YOUR RESPONSE: "What I'm saying and what I mean is... (Don't let reporters put words in your mouth.)

REPORTER: "Some people are saying..."

RESPONSE: "What people are you speaking of..." (Challenge the reporter's source)

REPORTER: "We all know that..."

RESPONSE: "We don't all know that' because it is untrue..."

REPORTER: "What if..."

RESPONSE: "I can't speculate, I can only give you the facts as we know them now..."

REPORTER: "Off the record, what about..."

RESPONSE: "I'd rather stay on the record. We don't have anything to hide..."

When You're Warned

When you have warning about a crisis or problem, whether it's a local council meeting with adverse actions expected, or a planned boycott, or whatever, your advance planning can help mitigate any negative effects. Here are strategies for dealing with anticipated negatives:

a. If you expect an attack, take the offensive yourself and put the attackers on the defensive.

b. State the peril of the alternative. In other words, when you know what the complaint against you is, state what the alternative is to what you are doing, if the alternative is worse. The side that presents the bigger peril wins.

c. Seek help. If the problem is larger than just your business, but affects your industry or line of work, bring in your trade association. It probably has its own action plan. And yours should tie into it.

d. In reacting to an event that's coming, and your story will help you, set the time of press briefings in the morning, if possible. This gives TV crews time—if the story is big enough—to prepare for evening news broadcasts.

e. Once you've weathered the crisis, make sure employees, customers, public officials, community leaders, and others have a full explanation of what happened and what you have done about it to ensure it won't happen again, if that's realistic. You can't assume they have the full story or the correct explanation by counting on news media coverage.

Index